STEPHEN TUROFF, born in 1947, widely respected healers working t surgeon', he receives dozens of pati centre in Chelmsford, the Danbury Healing Clinic. He also travels extensively, working in Israel, Germany, Spain and other countries around Europe. He lives with his wife in Essex, England.

SEVEN STEPS
TO ETERNITY

THE TRUE STORY OF ONE MAN'S
JOURNEY INTO THE AFTERLIFE

AS TOLD TO 'PSYCHIC SURGEON'
STEPHEN TUROFF

CLAIRVIEW
LONDON

Clairview Books
An imprint of Temple Lodge Publishing
51 Queen Caroline Street
Hammersmith, London W6 9QL

www.clairviewbooks.com

Published by Clairview 2000
Reprinted 2001

First published by
Elmore-Chard, London

A catalogue record for this book
is available from the British Library

ISBN 1 902636 17 1

Cover by Andrew Morgan Design
Typeset by DP Photosetting, Aylesbury, Bucks.
Printed and bound in Great Britain by
Cromwell Press Limited, Trowbridge, Wilts.

'There is no death—only change!'
J. Legget (died 1916)

I would like to thank all my friends of the seen and unseen world who have made this book possible.

Stephen Turoff

Preface

As a psychic, I have been privileged to have numerous encounters with astral dwelling souls. They have enlightened me in every sense of the word about their experiences in the planes after death.

When a soul first leaves its body, it falls into a sleep-like state and awakens on the plane of the astral world suitable for it. I am often questioned about this term 'plane', and the nearest answer is a 'state' of vibration. For example, sound waves; ultra-violet waves from the sun; rays from an electric lamp; all of these are invisible, each interpenetrating, yet do not affect or interfere with each other. So it is with the planes in the astral world.

Dwelling on each plane are the souls appropriate to live and operate there according to their spiritual evolution: 'In my Father's House there are many mansions.'

Recently I was lecturing on Remembrance Day. As I stood there considering my approach, I became aware of a young man. With my psychic vision, I saw him clearly and began to relay what he told me of his death in the 1914–18 war. 'My name is James,' he began, and went on to tell his experiences after death at the age of twenty.

On my journey home, I was still conscious of him. When I settled into my armchair to gather my thoughts, he again came close. We exchanged pleasantries, and I thanked him for helping me earlier with the lecture. We even shared a few jokes! Over the next few days I got to know this likeable soul well, and a bond developed between us.

One day he asked if I would consider writing a book about his life, not his tragically short one on our plane, but in the planes he has moved through since passing. 'You've picked the wrong one here,' was my initial reply. However, after much persuasion from Jim and with my insistence that he would have to help a great deal, I agreed to accept this challenge. I did not fully recognize, and perhaps just as well, what a major task it would be. Yet, I am glad I embarked on it because, as Jim pointed out, I was helping him as well as learning so very much myself.

I set aside a certain time each day, and painstakingly the book took shape. Before each session started, I first prayed for guidance, and Jim drew close. I sensed his slapping me on the shoulder and heard his special greeting of 'Ready then?'

You will find some discrepancy in style owing to the way Jim communicated the book to me. He placed pictures in my mind and left me to interpret them.

What follows are the direct accounts of Jim's passing from our earth plane and his experience in the life hereafter. Many times I have questioned the validity of my becoming the author of them! Some portions are like uncut diamonds, similar to Jim himself, a little rough around the edges. Other parts are more like pearls, pearls of wisdom from the guides and teachers who aided him. He soon discovered he had much to learn.

I have done my best to string together these rough diamonds and pearls, these gems; and I sincerely hope their beauty and truth will enhance your lives as they have mine.

S. TUROFF

1

I DIED IN THE BATTLE OF THE SOMME.

These were the first dramatic words James Legget communicated. He continued to explain his passing at the age of twenty.

It was August 1914. I was just eighteen years old when the war broke out. Like most youths, I was eager to join the army and was lucky enough to be accepted, or so I thought at the time. Little did I realize I would not be coming back.

In November of that year, leaving a home where I had been lovingly cared for, I went into the camp at Caterham. This I found rather hard because I missed the comforts of home. That autumn was to be one of the wettest I had ever experienced. We were bedded down in rough army tents with only an oilcloth sheet and a couple of blankets.

The wooden huts which were being erected for the winter were only in the early stages of construction. We were kept under canvas, sleeping on the ground, until quite late in the autumn.

New orders were posted telling us we were to move into the Chelsea barracks. This cheerful news gave us something to celebrate because it meant that we were to be billeted under proper cover. Having finished our basic training, the regiment was posted overseas where we put our training into action.

In the coming year I had many lucky escapes but lost numerous close friends on the battlefield before fate was to strike the final blow. By 1916 my time was fast running out. I was brought forward to the trenches. The Huns were shelling our lines and no-man's-land in front of them. We waited for the attack we knew would follow the barrage. There was fierce hand-to-hand fighting, but we beat them back with little loss on our side. The word went down the line that we were to counter-attack before the Huns could regroup.

As darkness approached, the battleground was silent, apart from a few exploding shells which lit up the night sky. I made sure to keep my head down because the Hun snipers didn't need much light to hit their target. Suddenly the whistle was blown, and the cry went up, 'Up and at 'em lads!'

We were full of the fighting spirit created by the unique comradeship only found in this kind of situation. This was the moment we had been waiting for. Bayonets fixed we surged over the parapet. It was no surprise to the Huns we were coming because they chucked everything at us except the kitchen sink.

As we advanced across no-man's-land, I was hit in the chest by a piece of shell. I lay on the ground in agony for hours. Dawn crept over the land, and I felt continuous waves of men stumbling over me as they went forward.

After a time I fainted from loss of blood. I came to later as the sun was setting. There was an uncanny mist that covered everything. I prayed a shell would hit me and put me out of my agony because the excruciating pain was too much to bear. Again I fainted. When I recovered I felt dazed but experienced little pain and no longer felt weak and tired. I put my hand to my chest to determine how much damage had been done by the shrapnel. To my amazement there was not a tear in my tunic. I hauled myself up with great difficulty because I was in complete darkness. Although they sounded distant, I heard the guns and clamour around me. After a while I became used to the darkness, which resembled a thick mist, and saw amidst it dark shadows flitting to and fro. Other shadows lay still. I decided to move on; I didn't want to get caught or to be cut off from the rest of the lads.

What happened next is difficult to explain. It was like a dream in which you try to move and are unable to. Something prevented me from moving more than one or two feet. I felt around and discovered a cord had attached itself to me in some mysterious way. I caught hold of it and tugged, but could not loosen it. I ran my hands down until I came to the place where it ended as an indistinguishable dark shape. This puzzled me a great deal and made me feel uneasy, even scared. I sat down to think things over.

Head in hands, I frantically tried to decide what to do next. Suddenly I heard voices close by and, on recognizing a friend, I called out to him; but no answer. As I pulled myself to my feet I shouted, 'I'm here!' The voices grew louder and two shadowy forms moved nearer.

'Look out!' I cried as they walked straight through me. They knelt down near the shadowy heap to which I was attached, and one seemed to be doing something to it. I was puzzled and thought I must be delirious, but at least they had found me. I suddenly heard one of the shadows cry out, 'He's gone, poor fellow, we'd better get him back.' I wondered about whom they were talking. They both bent down and to my amazement they picked up the shadowy heap to which I was attached. As they moved off I was pulled with them by this mysterious cord. I was screaming at them to stop, 'For Christ's sake, what are you doing? I can see you, I can hear you, why don't you answer me?' But this was to no avail.

Then the words of one of the shadows came flooding back: 'He's gone poor fellow.' I kept saying to myself, 'But I can't be dead, I can hear and see; maybe not very well, but I can see.' I hoped and prayed they were mistaken. They stopped by a low building and still held the shape to which I was attached.

A new voice spoke, 'Don't bring him here, he's been dead for a time. Put him round the back with the rest for burial.' I vaguely remember hearing the words of the burial service, then silence. The shadows turned to go, and for the last time I heard my friend's voice, 'He was a decent sort.'

The voices gradually faded into the mist and I heard no more. I slowly ran my hands over my body and face. I still had a body, but yet they must have buried something. By now the realization that I might actually be dead slowly began to dawn on me. I was terribly confused and afraid. I wondered what on earth would happen next. If I were dead, where was heaven? I began to cry uncontrollably and uttered, 'Dear God, please help me. I know I never went to church, but I always tried to be good.'

Strangely, my fear turned to anger. My whole body began to pulsate. I wanted desperately to be free from this cord and my anger gave me the strength to do something about it. I took hold of it and pulled. I can't easily describe how I felt next. There was a lightness in my body and mind. I felt clear for the first time since I'd been hit. I was now free!

I looked about myself and gazed across to where the cries of war were coming from. I could see many shapes running, falling. Some got up, others just lay there. I noted one in particular. As I watched, I saw a fine mist pour out of it and mould itself into the figure of a man who hovered above the dark shape. With astonishment, I assumed this must have happened to me. I then saw a completed figure which had a fine silver cord extending from it that joined the shadow below. I continued watching. The man began to stir and struggle. Obviously he was unable to understand what was happening, much as I had been. I thought, 'Poor sod, perhaps I can at least help him in some way or other.'

It didn't take long to reach him. As I approached, I heard his crying as he struggled. I shouted, 'Don't panic! I'll help you.' At the same time I was thinking, 'God knows how as you're much bigger than me.' He saw me and began to scream, 'Help me, mate, what's happened to me?' 'Well,' I said, 'I think we're dead!'

'Don't be a daft bastard,' he shouted. 'How can I be? I'm talking to you! How can I be dead? Everyone knows that when you're dead, you're dead.'

'Well, mate,' I said, 'just stop to think. Can you move from where you are?' Suddenly a look of horror crept across his face. 'No,' came his reply, 'I can't. Something's holding me. I think it's some type of line.'

I put my arms around his chest. 'Pull, come on!' I shouted. With one almighty heave, he broke free from the dark shadow lying on the ground. He came away from his dark shape much quicker than I had from mine. I don't know how or why, but he did. He was free, and so was I. Thus began our journey into the new life.

'My name is James, but my friends call me Jim,' I said to

him. He responded, 'Well old pal, I'm Bill, Bill Barnes. But my friends call me The Bear.' One look at him and I understood why. But in spite of his size, I saw the fear on his face and the bewilderment in his eyes.

'Let's talk,' he said. We walked on a bit as I explained how I'd come to this place and how I'd watched his arrival. 'It's ridiculous. I can't be dead!' said Bill. 'I've got a wife and three kids. What will they do without me?' 'I don't know,' I said, 'I just don't know. There must be an answer to all this.' We carried on walking.

'The way I see it, we can't be the only ones to have died. There must be others. By the way, have you noticed that it's neither light nor dark here, just misty? I don't know if it's day or night, or what time it is. Let alone what's happening.'

The ground underneath our feet was hard. The sounds of war diminished steadily behind us. We made our way through the mist. I stopped and turned to Bill, 'I think we're lost and I don't know which way to go.' But Bill wasn't listening, he was looking in another direction. 'What's up?' I asked.

'There's a light coming towards us,' Bill replied. 'Perhaps it's help.' Slowly the light grew in size, and I heard voices within it. 'Can you hear that Bill?' I whispered. 'Yes, I can. There are people behind the light. Look, there are several people here. Perhaps they can help.'

I called out, 'Hello, there! Can you see us?' 'Yes,' came the reply. An officer stepped forward with another gentleman who was dressed unlike anyone I had ever seen. 'Hello, sir,' I said. 'Could you tell us what has happened and where we are?' The officer replied, 'All will be explained later. First we have to move on from here.'

We followed the captain and the strange man who carried a light. As we walked, we stopped occasionally to gather others who were in the same situation as ourselves. As we walked further the mist cleared, and the earth became softer underfoot. The scenery began to change; trees came into view. There was no sun, but it was warm. As we continued I noticed rough, browny-green patches of grass and some partly demolished buildings which I assumed were remnants of the war.

We approached a large Nissen hut where a group of young soldiers waited nervously at the entrance. I turned toward Bill to ask what he thought of this. But, as he was smiling, I instead asked, 'What's so funny?' He answered, 'I'm just thinking. Is this where they dish out the wings and harp? If so, they'd better be pretty big for me!'

'Don't kid yourself, soldier!' a voice answered. We turned to see the captain standing there. He continued, 'You may have a pretty good idea of what's happened to you, but let me make it quite clear. All of us are dead, well, dead to the physical world anyway. I've been here quite a time helping people like yourselves adjust to a new home. I know you've got a lot of questions which I assure you will be answered. Now I want you all to go into the building, where you'll find seats. Just sit back and relax.' The captain moved off with the gentleman carrying the light.

We entered a large, noisy hall with hundreds of chairs, mostly filled with men but a few with women. Some people talked, others laughed or cried. Some just stared silently ahead. There was a rostrum at the front of the hall. I turned to Bill and said, 'I hope we get answers here to our questions.'

Suddenly music filtered through the air, and a hush came

over the hall. I can't describe the sound, but its effect was one of peace and calm. I looked across to Bill and saw the fear fade from his face. A peace came over everyone in the hall. After ten or twenty minutes the music stopped.

The voice of a tall officer rang out from the rostrum, 'Good-day ladies and gentlemen. My name is Marsh, and I want to explain where you are. You have noticed by now that something has happened to you. You have experienced a change of location, and also now realize this place is very real.

'You are in the intermediate stage between heaven and earth called the astral plane, but don't cloud your minds too much for the moment because it is a place of rest and adjustment. It will be like going back to school. You have much to learn here. This plane will have been a shock for many of you because you have seen that life is continuous. What you call death is simply a change of location.

'The hall you're in is one of many established within the lower astral plane to help those who die in battle. Here you are assisted in accepting this transitional stage of your new life. You may be wondering about the enemy. If this is happening to me, what of him? Well, God does not discriminate. You will come to understand later that all are his children.

'When you leave you will be split into groups and taken to billets. There will be someone assigned to your group who will talk to you about yourselves. You will then learn how to use your willpower, because it is the will of the individual that becomes potent in this life. I want you to look on the back of your chairs where there is a number which you must remember in leaving the hall. I will be addressing you again at a later date, but for now I will say good-bye.'

We made our way to an exit. I looked around to see where Bill was and caught sight of him just behind me. 'Alright Bill?' I asked. 'Sure, Jim. What number have you got?' enquired Bill. 'Would you believe 1901?' I replied. 'It adds up to my age. First we're given a number on entering the army. Now that we're dead, we're bloody well given another.'

I was interrupted by a shout, 'All those with numbers between 1900 and 1950, please follow me.' I looked up to discover that the voice belonged to a sergeant. I commented to Bill, 'We can't even get away from them here.' 'You're right,' said Bill, 'but I think we had better follow him.' We made our way across some fields and approached a large hut.

'Well, lads,' said the sergeant, 'you'll be billeted here for now. Inside you will find beds so make yourselves comfortable. I will be back soon.' On entering I saw beds on either side of the room and made for one of them while Bill took the one next to me. I turned to Bill and said, 'I think I'll lie down.'

I got on the bed and began to relax while thoughts of the last few hours passed through my mind which led me to think further back. I wonder if my Mum knows I'm dead. She will be heartbroken when she hears. She didn't want me to join the army, but I would not listen. Oh! Mum, I'm so sorry. If only I had listened, I would not be here now and unable to tell you that I am alive, yet dead. I felt myself sinking into some sort of depression when I heard the sergeant's voice. It was as if he'd been reading my thoughts.

'Right lads,' he said, 'may I have your attention? You have a lot to learn, and the quicker we get started the better. The first thing you're going to miss is those you love. This will take some time to get over, but with our help and your self control, you will master these emotions. I'm going to leave you now so that you can rest, but I will be back in a few hours.' With that the sergeant left.

I was very tired so I lay back on the bed and drifted off to sleep. I woke to the sergeant's voice. 'Wakey, wakey, rise and shine. Come on, you lot, get yourselves up.' I felt refreshed and calm after the sleep. When I got up I realized I was still wearing the same clothes I had on when I arrived, but strangely neither I nor they had any smell.

Bill called out to me, 'Are you all right, Jim?' I looked across to him, 'Yes, mate. I'm all right, but I wonder what they have in store for us next. How are you coping?' 'Not too bad,' he replied. 'It took me a little time to get to sleep, but I feel very good considering I'm dead.'

I remember saying out loud that he was a bit of a joker. Just then the sergeant called us to order, 'Let's have you outside now, in lines of twos. It doesn't do to keep the teacher waiting.' 'Well, here we go again,' I thought to myself as we marched.

I couldn't help noticing the look of apprehension on every face as we approached a church-like building. We went inside and took our seats. In front of us was an altar, table and two chairs. We did not have to wait long before the captain announced himself, 'Good-day gentlemen. Just in case you have forgotten my name, it's Marsh, Captain Marsh. I will not be addressing you myself but will hand you over to someone who has been in this world a lot longer than I, someone who has evolved to the higher planes of the astral world. What you are about to witness will come as a shock to you, but it is quite natural over here.'

All eyes centred on the captain and everyone wondered

what would come next. Suddenly a whirling mist appeared from nowhere. It began to shape itself into the form of a man and shimmered from head to foot as it solidified. In front of us stood a man where only a moment ago was empty space. I looked around for everyone's reaction. I think they were as amazed as I was. 'Gordon Bennet, what next?' I thought. 'Gentlemen,' said the captain, 'I now hand you over to the teacher.'

'Obviously, I have your attention,' said the teacher. 'I can't think of a better way of getting that than an impressive entrance. First, I want to speak to you about your new environment. You are on the fourth of seven astral planes. Each plane differs from the others by the manifestation, density, and velocity of its basic essence. Your physical body varies in a way that determines your spiritual growth, which is what your soul is always seeking. Many of you literally starve your souls and, for example, allow your minds to become entirely engrossed and dominated by materialism.

'The soul is always called on to look up, not back. It must carry hope and love at the helm of your life. This is not always easy. Even with effort you do not always live up to these ideals, yet to make an effort is always a step in the right direction.

'My dear friends, you have died in war, and your conscious minds have created hatred for the enemy as they have for you. But you are your thoughts, and these thoughts of hatred hold back your development. Your own worst enemy is you, not the soldiers you faced across the battlefield. It is in the battlefield of life where you must build your character in preparation for your next stage.

'As it is, you have been thrown into this world before your

time – like an apple that is plucked before it ripens. For many of you the experience of an untimely passing is just this – a bitter taste. So it is our wish to help the ripening of your individuality for your soul's development. Look no further than yourselves because many of the answers lie within.

'Now I would like you to concentrate on what I say. You have been told there are seven planes. Likewise you have seven bodies. One of these was the physical body which you discarded when you left the earth plane. Here on the fourth astral plane, your astral body is learning to vibrate in accordance with the vibrations here. These are finer and faster than those on the earth plane. This explains why things here are as tangible and real as on earth. We aim to help you adjust and harmonize with the vibrations of your new environment.

'You are on the second stage of your conscious life, and as the third and fourth planes are only slightly finer than the earth plane, it is our endeavour that you move on to the fifth plane. This will occur when you refine your mental and emotional vibrations. I come from the seventh plane where matter vibrates faster and is more refined than here. You may wonder how I am able to visit your plane.

'The answer is simple. I have learned to wind down my vibrations in order to work on the lower planes. By using my power of thought, I can wind down enough to materialize here and talk with you. Well, this is quite enough for your first lecture. You will recall these words when you begin to rethink your first lesson. There is no need to take notes here. May the Great Spirit bless you until we meet again.'

With these words the teacher began to dematerialize in front of us. When he had gone, I thought about his strange explanations. Many seemed to be out of a story book. I had so much to learn and felt I understood so little. The captain stood up and asked if there were any more questions, and a few hands went up.

The captain pointed to one young man, who stood up and said, 'My name is George Taylor. Is there a God, sir?' The captain replied, 'Yes, George. There is a God, and we will explain later about the God force which is within all things.'

He then pointed to someone sitting at the back who stood up and said, 'My name is Tom Richardson. Will I be able to see my wife and talk to her, sir?' I immediately felt a concern within this soul. 'Tom,' said the captain, 'you have been told you will be allocated a special guide who will teach you how to communicate with all your loved ones.'

Tom remained standing and cried, 'Well, that's not good enough. I want to see her now.' His head sank low into his hands, and he cried like a child. 'That's enough, soldier,' said the captain. 'Control yourself.' I sensed a strong will in the captain's voice but one tempered with understanding and sympathy. Tom lifted his head, 'I'm sorry, sir. I don't know what came over me.'

The captain said, 'I understand how you feel. We all go through this at some time or another. But I can assure you, you will be all right. I left behind two children, the eldest only five. But I am able to communicate with them and my wife using a spiritually aware person on earth called a medium.

'Your guides will include this information in your practical lessons in order to help you through occasional stages of remorse which most of you will experience. I think we had better stop now, gentlemen. If you would like to stand and move outside, you will find your sergeant waiting for you.'

After we were dismissed, we made our way back to our billets. I lay on my bed and tried to take in all that had been said. There was so much going on inside my head that I quickly tired. I closed my eyes and fell immediately into a deep sleep. When I woke, I had an increased sense of strength such as I'd never felt before. 'God, it's wonderful to be alive,' I thought.

I laughed aloud to myself, 'What am I talking about? I'm dead!' Yet I felt more alive than I ever had. I walked over to the window, looked out and thought it must never get dark here because it was still daylight. I went back, sat on the bed and easily recalled what the teacher had said earlier. This was strange because I had never had a good memory. I looked across at Bill, who still slept. Let him rest.

After sitting around for some time and feeling rather bored, I suddenly realized that I had not seen past the boundary of the hall. Surely there must be more. I made my way to the door and opened it quietly in order not to disturb anyone. I proceeded towards the church and kept it as a landmark so that I would not get lost. As I walked on, I felt a warmth that radiated from every direction. I looked up, thinking it must be the sun, but the sun was nowhere to be seen nor was there a cloud in the sky. I had not looked before, which now seemed very strange. But, then again, what wasn't strange in this place? As I walked further, I saw other people. Some were young couples walking arm-in-arm; obviously, they had come together since coming here. How happy they looked!

On reflection I remembered that I had never had a steady

girlfriend; but what I had never had I wouldn't miss. It was such a beautiful day I made my way to a nearby spinney. When I approached, I saw that the trees were fine and upright. Nestled at their bases were daffodils and bluebells which brightly flourished into a crescendo of colour growing side by side within the grass. The air was saturated with the sweet scent of honeysuckle and lavender.

The carpet of flowers before me was so inviting that I sat with my back against one of the trees and began to relax. I noticed the trees were in full bloom, mirroring my frame of mind. As I daydreamed I began to drift off to sleep, but was interrupted by a voice.

On looking around, I was amazed to discover an Oriental standing immediately behind me. 'Don't be afraid,' he said, 'I'm here to help you. Let me introduce myself. My name is Chan, and I have been nominated to work as your guide. Even though we're of different races, there will be no language barriers between us.'

I looked him up and down and admired his splendid clothes. The colours were vivid as though they were alive. I wondered where he was from. 'From the sixth plane where I live, of course,' he said.

'Hey, I never spoke. How did you know what I was thinking?' 'I can read your thoughts,' he answered. 'Here it's not necessary to speak. You too will learn to use your higher senses for speech.' 'But you're talking to me now?' I questioned.

'Of course I am. Although I can use the power of my mind, it does not mean I wish to lose the power of speech. There is a lot for us to discuss, but first, let me finish what we've started.

When you first came over to this life, you brought your personality and all of its experiences with you. One of those experiences was your ability to talk and communicate on earth. You will not lose your old experiences. You can't lose them because they are part of your character. Life is about building one's character, and experiences are the building blocks of the character.

'Could you imagine a God of love taking a four-year-old child out of nursery and putting him into university? The child would be totally lost because he would be unable to comprehend his new environment. In order to understand the university stage correctly, he has to go through nursery, primary and secondary schools first. The next stage is then automatic, and the quest for education follows smoothly. It is the same for you because you cannot go from physical death straight into the spirit plane. The adjustment would be too great for you. You are taken through the astral planes in stages. Each one educates you for the next. You will have to re-adjust your old ideas of earth schooling, but I will be your teacher and help you with learning new ideas.

'Your first lesson will be to learn how to focus your thoughts by concentrating your willpower. You then can communicate with other souls mentally. The way this works is that a Thought becomes the Line, and the Will becomes the Impulse. Just as on earth you communicate by telephones, here you use the will. By controlling your thoughts and willpower you will be able to receive and send messages. It is immediate communication. Until you have mastered it, you must use your voice box. The one you have been using for the last twenty years.'

I was surprised that he knew my age, and being inquisitive I asked how. 'Well,' he said, 'I can read the pattern of your life which tells me all about you, from the moment of birth until now.'

'God,' I thought, 'he knows all about me!' 'Keep calm,' he said, 'I can read your thoughts, Jim. You don't mind my calling you Jim?'

'No,' I said with a start, 'I don't mind, but what is this pattern-of-life business?' 'I think it's best,' he replied, 'that I don't go into it now.' Thinking back now, I recall how little I knew or understood at that time. Later Chan and I became like father and son.

'Now then, Jim, I want to talk to you about your sleeping habits. Please do not interrupt me. You will find many beneficial changes here. One is that you will require no sleep. The sleep you've had since coming here was one of conditioning. When your mother first held you in her arms and nestled you into her bosom you felt safe and secure, so drifted into the world of sleep in order to rest your tiny body after its entry into the world. Your body was an engine that needed food, water and rest to function properly. Sleep was necessary to renew the body, but often it was used to escape daily commitments. Many think that all their troubles will disappear with a night's sleep. Nothing is further from the truth.

'Do you realize you have spent a third of your life asleep? Although you have not needed sleep here, your mind has retained the conditioning patterns from its earth life. The physical body slows down in response to the human clock which indicates when rest is needed. Your clock will alter to the vibrations of this plane and slowly break down your conditioned mind, allowing more freedom. The next time you want to sleep say, "No". After doing this several times, you will break the habit and no longer require sleep. You'll feel just as well, if not better.'

'But I felt so full of energy after my sleep,' I said. 'Just stop to think,' he replied. 'You will no longer need sleep, but you will have the same energy as before. At times you will find it necessary to rest in order to digest what you have learnt, but sleep as you have known it will be unnecessary.'

My mind was full of Chan's words. 'I know this must be a silly question,' I said. 'Are you telling me that if I tell myself I don't need sleep, I will not sleep and will feel just as good without it?'

'I've just explained this to you,' he answered in a tone that left me in no doubt that he knew what he was talking about and that I should have listened more intently. He asked if I had any other questions. 'Yes,' I replied. 'Where can I get something to eat? I'm bloody starving.'

'I was waiting for that,' he teased. 'Do you remember what I was saying a moment ago about sleep? Well, the same thing applies to eating.' I was taken aback by Chan's words and yelled out, 'You don't mean I can't eat either?'

'There is a good reason for this,' he replied. 'The conditions of life on the higher spheres are more dependent on mental power than those of the earth plane. For instance, you have a body which is a duplicate of the one you had on the earth plane. You have lungs which fill with air. You have a heart which beats and pulsates. You also have a liver, kidneys and other internal organs, but they are not used in the same way as on the earth plane because here you do not eat coarse food which must be processed by the liver, kidneys, etc. Here we absorb food or fuel through the pores of our skin as well as through our breath. This is totally adequate for our well-being.'

'So,' I said, 'to eliminate these hunger pains I need only think that I don't need food?' A smile crossed his face as he nodded. 'Very good, young man,' he said, 'you are beginning to learn already. As you go along, it will become easier.

'You have only been here a short time and already you are questioning and thinking in a different light. You learn quickly because you have a quality of perception that many lack. This is because you came over at such an early age, and the material way of earth life had not become too deeply embedded in your consciousness. However, you need an adjustment period because of the way you passed. Nevertheless, I'm sure you'll succeed when you gain experience. And I assure you, you'll have that opportunity here. Come, let us walk. I have finished talking for the moment and want now to show you some of life here. Also we'll get new clothes for you.'

I felt excited at the mention of new clothes because I still had on my uniform and was rather fed up with it. We walked for half an hour or so before Chan pointed and said, 'We're going just over that hill. Another time I'll show you how to use your willpower to travel anywhere you wish. In other words, you won't have to walk anywhere you don't choose. You'll get there by simply thinking of the place and directing your thought there. As I said earlier, thought acts as a line, and, in this case, the will acts as a magnet drawing itself to the line. All very simple,' he chuckled quietly.

I saw an all-knowing smile spread across his face when he finished speaking. 'So much for me to learn,' I thought. 'All these things – talking without talking, no sleep, no eating and now I don't have to walk anywhere. God, what's happening to me?' I was pulled from my thoughts by Chan's command, 'Calm down. I can read your thoughts. It's not as bad as you think. You'll find that without the limitation of the physical body you'll have a much wider field of expression.'

We reached the top of the hill and saw a small town beneath us. I looked at Chan whose smile seemed to say, 'I told you so.' It didn't take long to reach the town. It was like many towns on the earth plane. There were guest houses and shops of all kinds. The big difference between this town and those on earth was that this town was much cleaner. There were no dirty streets and polluted air. It was peaceful, without the ordinary hustle and bustle of town life on earth.

The shop windows were very plain because, as Chan explained, man could not resist temptation. Once things are displayed in shop windows on earth, they must be had. We have no need of temptation here. I agreed with his thinking.

We came to quite an ordinary-looking tailor's shop. There was no clutter of rail upon rail of jackets and trousers. A rather superior looking man entered the room where we sat. I stood to attention, forgetting for a moment where I was. The tailor began taking my measurements and asked, 'What is it you'd like, sir? Any particular style or colour?'

'No, no, whatever you think best. Mind you, I do like the colour of that,' I said while pointing to an indigo in the open sample book. I was pleased with my decision to have the unique blue. Once the measuring was over we were told to come back in about three hours. I saw that Chan was also pleased with my choice, even though he would never admit it.

'We have other stops for more garments,' Chan said and gestured for me to follow. We picked and chose from numerous shops until I had four bags of new clothes. You may wonder how I paid for everything. When I asked about payment, I was told it wasn't necessary because everyone here worked for the benefit of others. I thought how much better this way seemed.

'Well, Jim, are you pleased with your new clothes?' asked Chan. I was delighted and said so. 'Good,' he replied. 'Now I want to take you to a place where you can bathe and change into some of your new clothes.'

After a while we left the town behind and came to some fields. In due course we came to a wood where Chan led me to a pool overgrown with bushes. Pushing these aside, I saw the pool was fed by a small stream. It looked very inviting; it was as if the water beckoned me. Chan also encouraged me, 'Get out of those old clothes and slip into the water.'

It took only seconds to get out of my uniform and into the water. I can't put into words the feeling that came over me on entering the pool. It was as if the water had a mind of its own. As hard as I tried to push myself under, I popped up again. Chan stood next to my uniform and seemed to be in a deep state of concentration. Even from a distance, I sensed his willpower. He gestured with his hands, whereupon a light began to emanate from one of his palms. The light spread over my uniform and within moments the light and the uniform had gone.

This startled me, and I immediately shouted out, 'What

have you done with my uniform? Where has it gone? I will get into trouble if I don't have it.' 'You don't need reminders of war here,' he barked. 'You left the war behind you on the earth plane, but your uniform was a part of it and still held negative vibrations which could affect you. It is time to get out and dress. I have laid out your clothes.'

'But I need a towel,' I said. 'No, you will not,' he replied. 'Just get out, and you will see what I mean.'

I hauled myself to my feet, taking care not to slip, and there I stood in all my glory. The water on me just slid off, and I was completely dry! A most remarkable feeling came with it. All my troubles had been washed away giving me a new lease of life. I walked over to where Chan had laid out my clothes and put them on. When finished, I looked for Chan. 'I am here, over here,' he shouted from a clump of trees.

I laughed to myself because he looked ornamental as he sat on a chair under one of the trees. There was a chair obviously meant for me next to him so I walked over and sat down. 'Well,' he asked, 'do you feel better?' I answered, 'As a matter of fact I do. I feel extremely good since my bathe. Why is this?'

'More explanation is necessary,' he said. 'You know that your new body is different from your old one. It is subjected more to etheric energies. Your body and everything else here is affected by these energies. Water is the most charged. I want you to remember something from the earth plane. Cars there required an energy store in order to run efficiently. Think of your body as a car which uses a battery. The astral body possesses an etheric energy store which needs to be recharged when run down. Normally you draw sufficient energy from the ether to maintain your body. Occasionally you will do a particular job that will drain you faster than you can recharge. Until you have learnt otherwise, you will need to bathe in one of the streams to speed up the recharging process. I have no doubt, when you gain practical experience, you will understand what I have been saying.

'Already you have seen you don't need a towel. Let me give you an explanation for this. Our bodies are made up of chemicals drawn from the atmosphere, but in a much more refined state. The higher vibrations and the greater amount of life force which continually passes through us make our bodies far stronger, though more buoyant than earth bodies.

'The plane we are on is much nearer to the God force than the earth plane; therefore we draw a tremendous amount more of it into ourselves. This applied to your recent discovery that your body could absorb energy from water without absorbing the water itself.

'Let me give you another comparison. Sometimes during your earth life, you will have washed your mother's windows. When you put the wet rag to the glass, you would have noticed that the water ran off the pane leaving a small residue. Here you don't get the residue but are left with a clean and recharged body. Now, does this answer your question?' 'Yes,' I answered. 'But what happened to my uniform, and how did you make it disappear?'

'You certainly have an enquiring mind,' he said. 'That's good because it means you listen intently to what I say. By using my willpower, I am able to affect astral matter. This means I can build or dissolve it back into its original elements. For example our chairs have been built this way. First, I had to think of the chair and hold the thought in my mind while focussing my will on the thought form. This brought the subjective view into the objective world by drawing objective matter into use. This is how we get most things in this world.

Now, to the reason why I got rid of your uniform. It was infected with thoughts of war. The hatred, death and destruction you built up towards the enemy affected the gross nature of your lower self. Your uniform was a part of you. Although it did not have a mind of its own, it came into contact with your thoughts and acted like a sponge soaking up the emotions of war. Thus a transmission was formed between the uniform and you. Though unseen, there was an effect on you which clouded your feelings with hatred of your fellow men. You must not allow this because it impairs your spiritual growth.

'This is one of the reasons we try to get new souls away from their immediate earth conditions, otherwise they continue the battle on the lower subdivisions of the astral plane where evil reigns. You were lucky to have been found by the captain and brought here, otherwise lower elements would have got hold of you and trapped you by the lower desires of earth life such as drinking, gambling and sex. You then would have become a slave to those desires and slowly sunk deeper into astral matter, creating your own hell.'

I was amazed to hear Chan mention hell. I asked if there was such a place and, if so, where it was. 'Another time I will explain where it can be found,' he said. 'Now I prefer to continue with what I was saying. There are heights for you to climb, but the first step starts at the bottom rung. The battle between good and evil is always waged on the lower levels. Sometimes evil tries to expand its boundaries, and open conflict occurs. It does not last long because we have the power of right on our side. At times the Lords of Light venture into the affray, and, with their help, evil is soon dispersed. This provides us with an opportunity to take prisoners, whom we hope to convince of the error of their ways.

'We cannot hold them long because their own evil thoughts pull them back to their plane. Sometimes the souls are not evil but are lost and have fallen into the wrong company. If they agree, we help them climb out of their darkness on to the path of light. The souls who work to uplift these lost beings are called rescuers. They have the task of going into the lower planes and are chosen for their highly developed willpower. To venture into the darkest of these realms takes a great deal of skill and courage. And in these darkest realms rescuers go in groups of four in order to maintain the four cardinal points of the soul they are helping. In this way evil does not stand a chance of interfering with our work. The retrieved souls are taken to a place of rest, where they stay until they develop a more positive attitude and until their minds open to the higher influences of life here.

'We have a whole army of souls who work in this way. I worked as a rescuer until I was placed in charge of your well-being. Now, it is time to get you back. I have talked at length about the way of life here, and you need to digest what has been said.'

We got up from the chairs, which disintegrated with a wave of Chan's hand. I asked if he would show me how to do this. 'Yes,' he said, 'another time. We must go.'

It didn't take long to walk back to the billet. I felt good and felt I looked good in my new clothes. 'When will I see you again?' I asked. 'Very shortly,' he replied. 'You need rest now. If you need me, concentrate on my face and name. And see what happens! Goodbye, for now.'

I thanked him for his help. He waved goodbye and suddenly started to fade. Within moments he was gone. I thought to myself, 'Can you beat that? Here one minute and gone the next.'

2

I opened the door to the hut and came face to face with Bill.

'Good God, Jim,' he said, 'you do look well. I like your new suit, very nice indeed. What have you been up to?'

'It's a long story. I never thought that life after death was anything like this. It's nothing like what Mother told me. She learned totally different things in church. Where are the guardian angels? The nearest I've seen to an angel is a Chinaman who comes and goes as he wishes. But he's a good sort and has been showing me the ropes.'

'Did you say a Chinaman?' Bill laughed. 'Yes I did,' I replied. 'What's so funny?' By this time Bill had to sit down from laughing so hard. 'When you've finished, tell me the joke,' I commanded.

'Well,' he said, 'if you can have a Chinaman for an angel, guess who I have?' 'I'm beginning to think anything's possible,' I said. Bill swallowed his laughter to speak. 'Listen to this. I have a Red Indian for a guide. He calls himself Medicine Man, and I've had quite a time with him I can tell you. He's promised to take me for new clothes later on. I'll look as smart as you then.'

This time we both burst into laughter. Who would believe we had a Red Indian and a Chinaman for guardian angels? We could not contain our fits of laughter. Finally everyone in the billet joined us, although they didn't know what they were laughing about. This went on for some time until I decided to lie down on my bed.

I felt cheerful and started to think things over. I wondered how long I'd been here; I'd lost all sense of time. The memory of my last battle had faded. Was it a day or ten days ago? God only knows, so much had happened in the meantime. A loud bang brought me from my thoughts; the sergeant stood at the door.

He looked around the room, shook his head and mumbled something about our appearance in a light-hearted attempt to make us feel guilty about being out of uniform. 'Right,' he said, 'there's a meeting with the captain. On your feet, move.' 'Here we go again,' I mumbled. We entered the hall and sat down. Bill sat next to me. As we waited for the officer's address, we shared a few jokes.

'Good-day, gentlemen,' the officer boomed out from the rostrum. 'I have heard that you are all settling in. That's good. Each one of you has been introduced to your guide whose job it is to help you learn the workings of this plane. I am sure it has come as a shock to many of you that your guides are of different races. All are God's children, and all of us evolve the same way. I now hand you over to the teacher.'

'Welcome, my friends,' began the teacher, 'I bring greetings from the Most High who looks on you all with love. I wish to address you about the God force that lies within you. For those of you who were agnostic in the earth life, it will have come as a shock that you survived death. And a greater shock that there is a God. Do not think of God as a man or woman who sits on a throne looking down from a great height to see if you are good or bad. Nothing could be further from the truth.

'God is the intangible spirit behind all life, his force is ever-present. God has bestowed life on you and crowned it with consciousness, knowing this would develop individuality. Thus it can be said that our gift from God is our own conscious individuality which cannot be taken away. You may well ask why you were not conscious of this in your earth life.

'From the moment you were born, you were surrounded by material things to sustain the material body and mind. As you grew up, the material mind created a concrete wall around itself because your concrete thoughts were conditioned that way. Once this wall is built, it stops some of the spiritual sunlight from entering your life. You become unable to recognize anything beyond the concrete world.

'There are some people on the earth plane who strive to recognize the God-qualities within themselves. In doing so, they slowly break down their walls allowing the sunlight of spiritual truth to enter. When this happens, they become aware of their true nature and try to use their knowledge of purity and love to help humanity by spiritualizing the consciousness of those they meet. There have been many such enlightened souls who have imparted their knowledge to a hungry world. One such soul was Jesus of Nazareth who portrayed the Christ-qualities of strength, love, goodness and compassion. Everyone he came into contact with was better for meeting him.

'My friends, you have the same qualities within, even though the Christ-light does not burn so brightly. You must endeavour to recognize this light and become aware of its power. You will, by your very thought, increase this divine power tenfold. We want you to realize your potential for good or bad. The power works the same for each.

'As a plant or flower exhales a pleasant or unpleasant perfume, man likewise influences his surroundings for good or for bad. You cannot meet someone without influencing his soul. You will be taught to control your lower thoughts and to exhale the higher ones because, in time, you will come into contact with others who need help. Just as we are helping you now, you also will stretch out the hand of friendship. But learning is a slow process for all of us because each soul has a different level of awareness and has embarked on an individual journey through life.

'I want each of you to consider what the word "life" means. Let me explain more clearly. You cannot destroy life. You can only change its mode of expression. The physical body doesn't exist after death, but the life force within that body will exist on another plane. It has simply changed location. There is still a body that lives, and a mind that thinks. You have experienced this transition yourselves.

'Now to the reason why you survived death. The life force, about which I have been speaking, is called the God Within. God cannot destroy himself because he is the natural law that surpasses all laws, including the law of physical death. The law of life is a continuum of movement and change. Nothing can hold back evolution because it is a must, and your evolutionary climb into higher and higher states of consciousness is your birthright given by the supreme being we call God. It is sufficient for now to have touched on this great mystery called life.'

The teacher paused for a few minutes and then asked if we had any questions. I looked around the hall and saw many heads turning to discuss what the teacher had said. The side discussions continued until one young man stood up and asked, 'Will I ever meet him, sir?'

'What is your name young man,' the teacher enquired, 'and whom do you wish to meet?' 'Well, God of course, sir,' he answered. 'Oh, yes! My name is Albert Ford.' Everyone laughed as the chap became flustered. I bet he wished the floor would open and swallow him. But to give him his due, he remained standing. 'That's enough, gentlemen!' the teacher said. 'Calm down now.'

A hush came over the hall and Albert sank back into his chair. The teacher continued, 'Albert, by getting to know yourself you get to know God. As I have already explained to you, he is within you. By understanding this, you will realize that God is within all things, and all things are within God. It cannot be any other way. The secret of life is life itself. In time you will understand this. And, when you do, you will say "I've met God". I hope this has answered your question, Albert.'

Several hands immediately shot up. The teacher picked another young man, who stood up. 'The name is Tom Adams, sir. My father died many years ago. If there is life after death for everyone, why have I not seen him?' 'How did he die?' the teacher asked. 'Supposedly of consumption, sir.'

'The way you died,' explained the teacher, 'has created a division between you and those who went before you. As you were cut off in the prime of your earth life, your spirit needs to adjust to its new environment. When you're ready, you will be able to come close to those with whom you associated while on earth.

'In your father's case, he would have been met by those who loved him. They would have welcomed him and immediately taken him to rest from the conditions of death. Once recuperated, he was educated to his new environment in the same way as you are now. When the time is right, the love you have for your father and the love he has for you will automatically bring you together. Where there is love, there cannot be a permanent separation. The law of attraction guarantees this.' I saw a smile cross Tom's face as he sat down.

The teacher had satisfied us by answering many of our inner questions and worries. He then thanked us and left as quickly as he had come. The captain approached the rostrum and began to speak. 'My thanks for coming, gentlemen. You can go back to your billets, or, if you wish, you may go for a walk. Don't wander too far, there's good chaps.' After the rush for the exits, I looked for Bill and caught sight of him heading towards the billet.

It was such a wonderful day that I decided to go for a walk. I headed away from the hall and soon came to the countryside. After crossing some fields, I approached a river. An uncanny light danced on the water. I sat to watch the lights and enjoyed their hypnotic effect. I discovered that when I concentrated my thoughts on the lights, they altered into images of my past. This entertained me for some time. When I became bored, I remembered Chan's last words: 'If you need my help, concentrate your thoughts on me.'

Immediately I formed a picture of him and added his name. Two to three minutes passed, and then a mist appeared. It formed itself into the outline of a man and became more and more solid each second. At last, Chan stood there in all his finery. He looked as splendid as when I last saw him, and I warmed to see his recognizable, all-knowing smile.

'Good-day, young man,' he said. 'Your power of concentration is very good. I received your thought immediately and was able to direct myself by it. The system works very quickly because thought travels instantly. I was in the middle of my meditation when you called, therefore I was able to come quickly.'

'Meditation? What is that?' I asked. 'I think I had better sit down,' he said, 'this may take some time.' With a wave of his hand Chan materialized a chair and sat down beside me. 'That's better,' he said. 'I see you have been looking at the lights of the water. What have you learnt from them?' 'I don't know, but I found them most enjoyable.'

'Yes,' he replied, 'you would because they are the lights of abstract thought. By concentrating on these lights you have started on the road to meditation. Since meditation is a key to heaven's door, let me explain more about its use.

'It is one of the ways to unfold the spiritual awareness deep inside the innermost part of your being. To develop that inner being, you must first come to know it and recognize its potential growth. Meditation is an aid to growth and helps develop the mind as well as the spirit. It balances the body you now have and the mental and spiritual ones you are creating.

'In your earth life, and now in this life, you educated the body to its environment. You must also educate the mental body. It must be trained, nourished, and made into a polished instrument for the spirit. To develop large muscles, one exercises to enlarge each muscle fibre. In the same way, we develop the mind by exercising the mental atoms. You must use your mind to peer into the depths. The more you see, the more you learn. Your reverence for the unseen will also deepen. When you were on the earth, the astral world was the unseen and your world was reality. Now our world is your reality, and you cannot comprehend the unseen world yet to come.'

I nearly dozed off so Chan stopped to ask if I were bored with what he was saying. 'No,' I said and pulled myself to. There was more authority in his voice as he continued; 'There will be a new meaning to life as you gain control of your lower thoughts and emotions. You achieve this by giving the higher mind food for thought, spiritual food that is. You strive to attain a purely spiritual illumination. To do this you will need a perfectly balanced mind and a well-controlled body to calm the mental vibrations which continually act and react with the spiritual level. With meditation you bring these forces under your control so that you become the master and not the slave. Has this answered your question?'

'I must be honest,' I said. 'I really don't understand what you've been talking about.' I saw a stern look cross his face and I waited for the telling off I knew would follow! 'You should have been listening more intently,' he said. 'I understand how difficult it is for you, especially since you have not been brought up in an eastern religion. In my old country, meditation was a way of life. I must make allowances for you. But please understand, these teachings are for your benefit.'

A subtle look crept over his face which said, 'You will learn.' We sat and talked for some time, and Chan explained more about meditation. This time I listened more carefully. I had lots of questions, and Chan provided the answers until he decided he had spoken enough on the subject.

'Well, my young friend,' he said, 'it has been a good day, and you have done extremely well. Now my job must concentrate on the practical side of your teachings. There will come a time when you will venture out on your own and work to uplift souls who are on a lower level of vibration than yourself. The plane below this one is denser, and evil gravitates there. Strengthening of your willpower is an essential part of your development because it will guard you against the evil influences of the lower plane. You were very lucky not to have fallen into the clutches of evil when you passed over. I did not intend to talk to you about the lower planes, but I think as we are on the subject, I will continue.'

With a wave of his hand Chan produced a parchment. As he unrolled it, he called me over for a close look. He thought it good to show me how the planes of the astral world correspond with each other. The drawing was very impressive, and I studied it for some time. But to be honest, I could not fully understand it and asked Chan to explain it.

'Well,' he said, 'there are seven planes and each one varies in density. Each plane is inhabited by souls suited to it. This is determined by the vibrations of their astral bodies which are controlled by their manifested thoughts. The astral plane, as you know, is semi-material. It also has something similar to space and position. Time also exists though in a more fluid form than on earth. Each of these planes has many divisions known as time zones which house souls who belong to that period of time. Many of those souls are able to travel from one time period to another, but most are happiest in familiar surroundings.'

I interrupted Chan by asking if he lived in his own time period. 'Yes I do, when I get the chance,' he replied. 'My work is mostly in this time period. You will find in this plane's divisions that the inhabitants are less graded and sorted out than in the higher planes. On this plane, life approximates closely to life on earth. Yet you will find men of different nationalities discussing abstruse problems by means of telepathy, nearly as completely as we do on the higher planes. There are two planes that I have yet to talk about. These are the two lowest where there are no divisions. They mould into one. I will use an example.'

With another wave of his hand Chan materialized an onion which he said was perfect for his demonstration. He held it in front of me and began to explain the significance of the onion. 'The centre core is the densest part. Imagine the astral planes in the same way. The centre is the densest form of matter, and each layer outside the centre is consecutively finer and bigger.

'The earth plane is the third division as seen by us, and evil reigns supreme over the two below the earth. The first plane is frequently talked about in your churches and is called 'hell'. It is a negation of all that is totally good and is the battleground for the evil passions that sink there from earth. At times the sheer force of these evil passions becomes personified. It sends roots deep into the second and the third planes. These roots feed on the evil passions and hatred generated by war. The forms arising from this evil are often seen on the battleground. One such form is the Angel of Death. The living and dying see it as a large shadowy figure which blots out the sun as it covers the battlefield. It becomes stronger and bigger as the emotions of war increase.

'It is in wars, such as this one, that evil in its lowest form pushes its way out of hell and overflows into the second and third planes. The roots of evil tap into the power of the Angel of Death and replenish its power as it pushes to dominate other planes. The newly slain are also used by the evil elements in its climb out of the pit of hell.'

A shiver came over me as Chan described the evil of these lower planes. To think I too could have been used! I remembered that Chan had remarked about hell before. 'You mean to say hell really exists?' I asked. 'That is what I have been telling you,' he said. 'I have not ventured into the first plane, but I have worked within the boundaries of the second. What I witnessed was extremely upsetting. I have talked enough for now on this subject.'

Before Chan could utter another word, I asked him if he would continue. I was captivated with what he had been saying. He continued, 'Well, if you wish, I will describe what I witnessed there. It is a place where evil mortals sink into their various sins of obsession. These souls wander aimlessly around in the mire they have made for themselves. A dense mist covers everything. There is no landscape and no buildings; instead there are great canyons where degenerate mortals lurk as they fast drift into hell. They live in slimy, filthy shelters between the rocks. There are no animals because the souls of animals cannot sink to these depths.

'The souls are there by their own making and desires. At times, when evil is on the march, it uses these degenerate mortals as its army of darkness. Darkness cannot hide from the powers of light, but it can from the newly slain. It can also hide from those on the earth plane by disguising itself to take advantage of man's lower emotions. This is done in the same way that an actor dresses differently for his roles in different plays.

'Although they are dead to the earth plane, these degenerates crave the pleasures of the body. They are certainly alive on the plane where they are. Their desires are much stronger than when they were on earth. They are linked with a mass of like-minded souls, thus creating a powerful driving force. This will eventually spill into the earth plane and prey on human beings still in the flesh.

'Their victims will be of like mind. For example, those who practise the black arts will be victims of their own desires. Those who are always drunk and the lower types of criminals will become victims of these obsessive souls. They entwine themselves with their victims in order to gratify their own burning desires. You see many of these beings crowded around drinking dens and houses of ill-repute. They wait to enter the aura of their victims. I know I have not spoken to you about auras yet, but I will.'

I could not move a muscle. Every part of my body was tense with fear. Chan asked if he should continue. Without hesitation, I answered in the affirmative. 'When the degenerates gain entry into the aura of their victims, they stay until they are shaken free. This can be accomplished by the individual himself or by an exorcist. If freedom is not achieved, the entity takes control of the earth body by dominating the weak soul's personality. Possession now occurs, with an ensuing fight for expression. First the earth soul hears voices which tell him to do things that are against his better judgement. The voices are so dominating that the weak soul can only obey by acting completely out of character. When the possession gets too bad, a doctor is generally called. In the worst cases the patient may be institutionalized. Out of desperation, doctors often call this condition schizophrenia and certainly have no real idea of the problem.

'Do keep in mind that all those who drink or indulge in the gratification of the body are not always evil people. Some are weak-willed and are led by those who are themselves led by evil. It was my job to go with others to find these lost and bewildered souls and explain to them they were making conditions for themselves which would be hard to overcome. We also try to explain that they are being used by a much more malignant force, and that if they do not turn from their path, they will be lured into hell. Generally this gives them something to think about. We call this the placing of the seed, and hopefully it will take root. We want them to see the light and find themselves.

'Nobody is ever lost or can be lost, because the spark of life is within all. But he can sink so low as to be nearly extinguished. At times, evil beings attack us if they think we are having success with one of their legions. This is why you are taught to control your willpower, because it is your will that guards you and keeps you safe. You will learn never to be afraid. The greatest enemy is fear itself, so you must be confident in the love and wisdom of God. Darkness will not touch you if you radiate light. Thus, by the power of will we are able to send the evil beings back to their own plane to be submerged in evil passions.

'I have now explained a little about my work before I was assigned to your well-being. This helps explain why I was chosen to be your teacher. You too have the quality and strength to become a rescuer.'

'Not bloody likely,' I said as I jumped up to stretch my legs.

A broad grin came across Chan's face. 'Well, we will have to wait and see,' he said. 'Would you care to take a chair?' 'Yes,' I said, 'the ground is rather hard.' With a wave of his hand, another chair appeared. I thanked him and made myself comfortable.

He continued, 'When evil pushes into the third plane, there is a confrontation between the forces of good and evil. We battle to send the evil forces back. Sometimes evil is very strong and pushes us back, but not for long. We call for help from higher souls who in turn call the Lords of Light into the fray. With their help, we push the evil army back. In the confusion to hide from the light, their army becomes a shambles, but it does not end here. The Lords of Light chase them from the earth plane into the second plane. Their light confuses all who are evil, and the beaten army is no more.

'When you passed out of your physical body, you saw something of the third plane. That is where your story began. For new souls, it is a misty place of thoughts and reasons. There are other planes, as I have stated. You are on the fourth plane and are in a time zone appropriate for your well-being. You are learning how to adjust to your new life. And, as you gain knowledge, you will become more conscious of your true self and of the God force within.

'Soon you will be preparing for your next stage of existence. As the vibrations of your mental atoms increase, your astral body will change. Just as a butterfly breaks free from its cocoon to emerge into a new world, so will you. It is a slower process with you than with the butterfly, but your new world is much more refined. This process occurs on all the planes from the first to the seventh. Each plane has the correct conditions for its growing souls.

'Now, let me tell you something of the plane where I live. It is the sixth, bordering on the seventh, which means I am getting ready for my birth into the heavenly sphere. This is similar to your death on the physical plane and your rebirth on to this one. Through my work, others have been uplifted and I have also earned rebirth for myself. This is the only path to follow. In time, you too will find the correct work. Do you remember the tailor?' 'Yes, I do,' I answered. 'He was a very helpful man. I meant to ask you about him and the place where he works.'

Chan began this story: 'That soul worked all his life as a tailor and loved his work. He enjoyed meeting people, and, because of this, his days on earth were happy. When he came over here, he still wanted to work. It would have been no good to put him into another occupation. He was given the task of clothing new souls until they can create their own clothes. Most people still have the desire to work. Although when they first come here, their reaction is often, "Thank God, I don't have to work any more." This does not last long because throughout life they have been conditioned to work. After a well-earned rest, they are introduced to a job that gives them a great deal of pleasure. Everybody works in one way or another, but here the work is carried out without payment. It is given in love as most people enjoy their work. It is a means of carrying the weight of their own responsibilities.'

'I understand this,' I said. 'I would become bored if I had nothing to do but sit around all day. Do you mind if I ask a question?' 'Not at all,' he replied. So I asked, 'Those shops we visited, how did they get there?'

'A good question,' he answered. 'The town and the shops exist on the earth plane. We have copied them so the new souls will immediately feel at home. To deprive them of the things they knew and understood when on earth would create a mental imbalance. So we are very careful to create an environment similar to the one they have just left. Of course, there are much greater things here than towns, houses and churches. Your country also exists! England is still England. A map would show that China too is in the usual place. The only difference between the earth and here is the way we live.

'Remember, Jim, what I said about distance? By using will and thought, I can travel from one place to another on the opposite side of the world in only a moment. Thus distance is overcome by controlled thought. We will continue shortly with a lesson in controlling your thought.

'The teaching guide to whom you were introduced lives on the seventh plane. He is a wonderful soul who works solely for the uplifting of humanity. He has evolved beyond the seventh plane into the spirit world. As he wishes to continue his work on the lower planes, he must remain under the manifestation of the astral planes, which differ from the spirit plane.

'All astral matter ceases to exist on the spirit plane, and only pure spirit functions there. The dividing line between the two is very fine, but, I can assure you, working towards the spirit plane is a worthy goal. There are many souls who hold back their evolutionary stage in order to help others. In my case, I have a long way to go. Have you any more questions?'

'No, thank you,' I said. 'Good,' he replied, 'we will start your training now. If you would like to get up, we can get rid of these chairs.' I pulled myself up and moved from the chair;

and, with a wave of his hand, the chairs disappeared. As before, I found this intriguing and remembered that Chan had said he'd show me how to do it.

'Right,' he said. 'First we will visit your billet. It is a good opportunity to start using your own steam for travel. Think of the place you wish to be and hold that thought in your mind. Next place your willpower on the thought and pull. Try it, Jim.'

'Right-oh,' I said. I closed my eyes, thought of my billet and found it easy to picture immediately. I started to pull myself on to my thought. A sense of lightness swept over me, followed by a peculiar feeling of movement. Yet, as far as I could ascertain, I had not taken one step forwards. It must have startled me because Chan shouted out, 'Stop! You look like a frog out of water. That is not the way; now try again. Concentrate more this time.'

'Well, here goes,' I said. I pictured my billet and con-centrated my will on it. This time I held the picture firmly in my mind. Again I felt myself moving. It felt more like riding on a bumpy train than flying through the air. My curiosity got the better of me, and I opened my eyes. This was the worst thing I could have done because I lost all concentration and im-mediately fell. I came down with a bit of a bang but was lucky to land among some bushes. As I pulled myself up, I caught sight of some young ladies standing near me. 'Good-day,' I said as I brushed myself off. 'I thought I would drop in.' This brought fits of laughter. I too saw the funny side of what I had said and joined in. One of them spoke briefly to me; 'We can see you're new here, but keep trying.' They turned and went on their way.

'So that is where you are,' a voice called. I turned to see

Chan's smiling face. 'So what went wrong?' I asked. 'Quite simply a loss of concentration,' he said. 'This is something you must not do if you wish to move anywhere by the power of thought. As to where you are, look around.' I did as Chan suggested. 'Hmm, it looks like a park,' I said.

'That is exactly right,' he replied. 'You overshot your destination. Your billet lies two miles in the other direction.' 'Oh dear,' I uttered, 'how did I manage that?' I knew full well what I had done wrong but was not about to say so. 'Well, what do I do now?' I asked. 'Try again of course,' he said, 'but this time do not open your eyes.'

I went as red as a beetroot, fully forgetting that Chan could read my thoughts. 'Do not worry,' he said, 'I did not expect you to get it correct the first time. As a matter of fact, you have done extremely well. Are you ready to try again?'

This time I did exactly as I was told. I held the thought of my billet firmly in my mind, and this time I kept my eyes tightly closed. As quickly as the moving feeling began, it stopped. As I opened my eyes, I was met by my old friend. 'Where in the world did you come from?' Bill asked with a look of disbelief as he pulled himself up from his bed.

'I've done it, Bill, I've done it!' I cried. 'I've come here without walking through the door.' 'Yes, I can see that,' he said. 'It's nice to see you again. You seem to be coping well with what has happened. I'm pleased for you.'

There was a quiver on Bill's lips as he lay back on his bed. This worried me so I moved closer to him to find out if I could do anything. I was startled by a hand on my shoulder and Chan's voice saying, 'Leave him, he will be alright. Come, take hold of my arm. I have a surprise for you.'

'Surprise, what surprise?' I asked. He lifted his hand towards me, and when I took hold, he said, 'Close your eyes.' A moving sensation began within moments. Only this time it was much stronger than I had experienced with my own efforts to travel. I sensed Chan's total control. As quickly as the feeling had begun, it ended.

'You can open your eyes now,' he said, 'and tell me what you see.' Slowly I opened my eyes, only to find myself in a mist. 'Where are we?' I asked. 'Use your power of concentration to clear away the mist,' explained Chan.

Once again I closed my eyes and used the full force of my willpower to clear the mist. I smiled and gave myself a pat on the back. At least I did it right this time. I found myself in very familiar surroundings and immediately recognized my old home. I wandered around the room; nothing had altered. The table was in the same place, and the sideboard was still underneath the window. I turned and asked Chan, 'Why have you brought me here?'

'Wait and see,' he said. The handle of the door turned and in walked my mother. Tears immediately formed in my eyes. With arms outstretched I rushed towards her, but I went straight through her. I turned for Chan's help. He mentally commanded me to stop. This was the first time I heard someone talking inside my head. It was not to be the last. I stopped on the spot, and Chan came across to me because he saw I was getting into quite a pickle.

'Calm down, my friend,' he said, 'your mother cannot see or hear you. The bond between you goes beyond physical death, and, in a mother's way, she knows you are here. Now we will have to go until you learn to control your emotions. On these visits you will have to adjust to your parents' emotional vibrations because they are still grieving for the loss of their only son. It is this grief that disturbs the ether around them. It is the sadness of their thoughts that affects you as you enter their mental area. I have kept you from these conditions to give you time to adjust and to become stronger in yourself.

'If you had come straight here from the battlefield, you would not have wanted to leave. Eventually you would have decided to leave but would have been unable to break away from the vibrations of your family. Your home then would have become a prison, with you earthbound to the emotional conditions there. Without help from one such as I or from a medium working in conjunction with us, you might have been trapped in your prison long after your parents' deaths.'

Chan stepped forward and placed his hand on my shoulder. Within moments we were back in the billet. It seemed we had never left, but I knew that for those fleeting moments of memory I had been back with those I loved.

'Well, I said it would be a surprise for you,' remarked Chan. 'It was not meant to upset you but only to prove that you can visit your loved ones. In time you will be able to travel to the earth plane whenever you wish. First you must gain more self control and, of course, more willpower. I will leave you now so that you can rest and think over your first steps of freedom.' Chan stood aside, and within moments he had gone.

3

I looked around the room hoping to find someone to talk to. But no, I had the place to myself. I moved to my bed, lay down, and started to think over Chan's last words: 'Your first steps of freedom.' He must have been referring to my first pathetic attempt to travel to the billet. I thought about my mother and my pleasure in having been given the opportunity to visit her. I longed to hold her, to tell her that I was alright, and that there is no death. Oh, Mum, if only you could have seen me, I have so much to tell you.

My thoughts tumbled back to childhood. My mother loved to fuss over me, especially when I was ill. Possibly because I was an only child, I knew just how to get around her. She always bought me the things I wanted. When she was angry with me, I nestled my head into her neck and said I was sorry.

Unknown to my mother and me, this type of behaviour placed me in a very delicate position, weakening me to everyday life. This was especially true at school, where everyone picked on me because I would not fight back. I ran home from school and hid in my father's potting shed. I felt angry with myself for allowing them to pick on me. The potting shed became my fortress and haven. I thought of all the things I would like to do to the bullies. I promised myself that, when I grew up, no one would hit me again. In my teens I learnt to look after myself. Surprisingly, I discovered that many of the bullies wanted to be my friend.

Mum was always her caring self and fussed over me whenever she could. She believed that cleanliness was next to godliness and made sure I had new clothes. We were luckier than most other families because Dad had a good job as a foreman carpenter. He wore a dark suit with a waistcoat and made sure his pocket watch always kept accurate time. His bowler hat went everywhere with him. When asked about his hat, he would reply, 'Sign of respect, lad.' He was a typical Edwardian father. You never answered him back.

I lived a quiet life until war broke out. Then everything became panicky. Friends and relatives were called up for the army. There were posters everywhere declaring, 'Your country needs you. Join now.' I was eighteen years old when the war started. I didn't know what the world was about, let alone how to fight a war. Nevertheless, I was eager to join up.

I explained how I felt to my father and stated the reasons why I wanted to join the Grenadier Guards. 'Let me think about it,' he said. When I looked towards my mother, her head was bowed low, and I knew what she was thinking. I left the room and went to the pub for a pint. I was there for some time talking with my friends about the war. When it was closing time, I made my way home. On entering the house, I made sure I was quiet since it was late.

I heard my mother's voice and stopped to listen. 'Harry, what is going to happen to our son now that war is looming over us. I don't want him to join.' 'Now, Mother,' my father replied, 'if it's God's will for him to be accepted into the army, he will have to go. He is no longer a child, and every man must do his duty for his country.'

I heard sobbing as I went to my bedroom. Mum loved my

father and me deeply and would do anything to hold on to both of us. Dad had a different attitude towards life. He commanded and received respect, but, underneath his hard exterior, he was a most devoted father. He was the head of the household, but it was my mother who made sure everything was where it could be found. If anything had happened to her, Dad would have been completely lost. He could not cook a dinner, let alone make a bed.

Weeks passed. In late October I received a letter telling me I had been accepted into the Guards and to report to Caterham by the sixth of November. The few days I had left were passing too quickly. Mum asked if I would go to church with her. She knew I didn't like going, not because I didn't believe in God, but because I thought it was soft. In addition, I wanted to spend whatever free time I had with my friends. I worked five and a half days a week so had very little time for myself.

I knew Mum was determined I should go, so I agreed. The vicar nodded when he eyed me in the congregation. He must have been taken aback on seeing me. I listened to the sermon and sang a few hymns. When it was over, my mother knelt and, with tears rolling down her cheeks, prayed 'Dear Lord, look after my boy.' I knelt next to her and put my arm around her: 'I'll be alright. Honestly, I will.'

The day came when I had to say goodbye. My parents took me to the station, and I was on my way after plenty of hugs and tears. 'I won't forget to write,' I shouted back as the train gathered speed. There were others in the compartment who had either joined up or had been called up to fight for King and country. I'm sure if any of us had known it would be the last time we'd see our loved ones, we would not have gone. But

I've learnt since coming to the next life that one's participation in events like war is predestined. I wrote several letters to my parents describing my progress and the battlefield tragedies. The rest is history.

My thoughts were interrupted by someone violently shaking my bed and saying, 'Get up, you lazy so-and-so.' There was only one person with such a deep voice. I looked up to see Bill standing there dressed up to the nines. 'Well, Billy, you certainly look the part, and that's a nice suit you've got. What have you been up to?' I asked.

'This and that,' he said. 'I went to the shops and got a couple of things, then sat and talked a great deal to the Indian fella. He's certainly an interesting bloke. We talked at great length about this place. By the way, where did you go? You were here one minute and gone the next.'

'I was taken to see my parents,' I said. 'It was certainly a surprise, and was the last place I expected to visit. Just seeing them gave me a lift, but it also brought back memories. I miss them, but now I know one day we will be together again. In the meantime, I have my memories.'

I felt myself becoming remorseful, so I asked Bill if he'd come for a walk, saying 'I know of a park not far from here.' 'I'd love to,' he said. 'Just give me two minutes to change my shoes, and I'll be with you.'

We headed in the direction of the park and stopped only once to ask directions. Soon we stood at the park gates. Once inside, the scenery was completely different. The grass looked and felt like velvet. I looked back and noticed there were no footprints where we had walked. I stopped and slowly lifted one foot. The grass was remarkably buoyant; it sprang back as though I had never trodden on it. There was an abundance of flower beds laid out to spell the word 'welcome'. The scent of the flowers was enchanting and made me feel peaceful and happy.

I turned and asked Bill if he felt the same. 'Yes, I do. What a lovely place,' he remarked. 'I wonder how they managed all this?' 'I don't know,' I said, 'but let's walk on.'

There were many people in the park, some arm in arm, others in groups debating. As we passed one group of young ladies I overheard a rather heated discussion. Just like a woman, I thought. They seemed to be the type who forever demand equal rights. I remembered it took all sorts to make a world. This place must be no exception. We continued our walk and, after some time, came across a hut. The door was open, and, being inquisitive, I stopped to look in.

Sitting there was a chap potting some plants. A gardener, I suppose. He seemed happy at his work. He turned and greeted us, but not in the usual way because he didn't move his lips. Instead his voice echoed inside my head. I immediately turned to Bill and asked if he heard it.

'Yes, I did,' he said. 'His voice was inside my head. How on earth did he do that?'

'I experienced this once with Chan,' I replied, 'but I thought everyone on this plane used his vocal cords to speak.' As the gardener stood up to push his stool under the bench, he smiled and made an aside on keeping things tidy. He turned and again spoke to us, but this time in the normal way.

'You are wrong, my young friend, to think everyone here speaks only through his larynx. Many can and do use both techniques to communicate. In my case, I get pleasure out of cultivating the park, as well as cultivating my mind. And practice makes perfect. Now, what can I do for you gentlemen?'

I think Bill and I had the same question in mind because we spoke at the same time, but I finished: 'How did you make the park so nice?' I asked. 'It must have taken ages to create such beauty.'

'First, I did not create the park,' he replied. 'However, I was instrumental in finding the right location. The rest was done by souls from the seventh plane whose willpower created the park. The sole purpose of this park is to provide recreation for people such as yourselves. Although I work on this plane, it's not my home.' I blurted out, 'I thought as much, you're not one of us.' I blushed when I realized what I had said.

'Don't worry,' he said, 'I know exactly what you mean. You're right. I'm not of this plane. There are many ways to work, and this is my way of helping. It's a job that I love. I have tended this park for many years now, and every day is like the first.'

'That's very interesting,' I said, but I was eager to ask how the park was created. The gardener must have heard my thoughts, because he interrupted with an explanation of the origins of the park. 'It's all based on love,' he said. 'It was love that brought it into existence, and it is through love that it is held in the form you now see. If there were a disintegration of that love for a moment, the park would fade into its natural elements. Higher souls are able to create in a finite way, but of course, not in an infinite way. Only God can hold his creations for infinity. Would you like to see something of the park?'

'Oh, please,' I said, turning to Bill who nodded his approval.

As we walked through the park I noticed there were no paths. The grass was an unearthly colour and texture. Groups of trees were dotted here and there. We passed many flower beds, and each was more beautiful than the last. The atmosphere was filled with a heavenly scent which filled my every breath with peace. My thoughts reflected over all Chan had told me. He was right; God is all understanding. I marvelled at this demonstration of the nearness of the unseen God.

'That's a good way of putting it,' said the gardener, 'I've been listening to your thoughts.' I forgot he could read our thoughts. I felt in a bit of a daze as he explained more about what I had been thinking. Later I became used to this. We walked towards a spinny of oaks in varying shapes and sizes. The gardener asked us to wait, and he headed in the direction of one of the trees. We watched curiously when he placed his hands on it. I saw from where we were standing that he conversed with it for several minutes. When he made his way back to us, Bill asked what he had been doing.

'Talking to the tree,' he replied. 'I see you have not yet been taught to commune with nature.' Bill smiled and interjected, 'Talking to trees, what do you mean, mate?' There was an added strength in the gardener's voice as he answered Bill with a lecture on God's law of creation.

'First,' he said, 'my name is not mate, it's Ben. And yes, I communicated with that tree. The spark of life within us is in trees as well, but of course, not at the same stage of evolution. You will learn that spirit can and does communicate with spirit at all other levels. Remember this park is built on love, and its plant life is extremely beautiful because of this. All God's creations respond positively to love. The tree back there felt my love. Of course, I cannot have a conversation with it as I can with you. Yet its twilight consciousness understands my thought and responds by perfecting itself to please others. When you thought, "What magnificent specimens", they grew to that thought. Now gentlemen, if you would care to follow.'

We walked past indescribable scenery. Its beauty surpassed any earthly idea of heaven. After walking about twenty minutes, we came to a large flower bed. It was one mass of colour; each flower blended with the next. None were out of place. It was a gardener's dream. The scent from the bed was heavenly, and triggered a stream of exotic thoughts. I turned for Bill's reaction. As I expected he had a faraway look on his face. I realized his thoughts had taken him back to an important part of his life, a happy part I hasten to add. 'Are you alright, Bill?' I asked. A sigh came from his lips.

'Yes, Jim,' came his reply. 'The scent has a magical effect on me. It makes me think of all the good things that happened in my life. I cannot remember one bad experience. I am very happy to be here. Who would have thought this place existed? If people knew of this place, they'd want to come before their time. That would not be wise because everything seems to have a purpose.' 'I know just what you mean,' I said. 'If everyone wished to join us, there would be no one left on earth. Perhaps there would not be room here for all of us.'

Ben entered the conversation, 'You are quite correct. The flowers have a hypnotic effect which permits one's soul to see only the beauty in one's life. In a short time you will be out of the mainstream of negative thought. Nothing has been overlooked in the creation of this park, from the grass you walk on to the air you breathe. Everything is in perfect harmony. You will begin to hear a calling within yourself to come higher. The calling will stay with you as a carrot in front of the donkey.'

'That's very interesting,' I said, 'but would you explain more about its origins?' Bill chirped up, 'Yes, please do.' 'I'll try to make it as simple as possible,' Ben said. 'As I said earlier, the park began with love. It attracted to itself like-minded beings who are very evolved and able to use their willpower to create much beauty. First there was an idea which led to the desire to create. Already the thought began to take shape. It then attracted even higher souls who added their power to achieve the desired shape.

'When the plan was finalized, a blessing was offered for its completion. First the group created a mental picture of the plan and held the image until it was as perfect as possible. The combined willpower of the group brought the subjective view of the park into the objective world where you saw it. You must remember that this plane is yours not theirs. This makes it more difficult for them to maintain the concept of the park, even though they are well versed in spiritual and mystical thought itself. I hope this has answered your question.'

Bill turned to me with raised eyebrows. I sensed what he was thinking and said, 'That will need digesting.' Ben chuckled. 'Don't get too confused. You will understand all I've been saying when you gain experience. Do you like music?' 'Oh, yes,' I said. 'Good,' he replied. 'There is a magnificent bandstand I wish to show you.'

We crossed the park. Ben pointed to some trees and remarked on them as we passed. Soon we came to a hill with the bandstand perched on top. Although there was no sun, it glistened like a diamond. I was looking forward to some music because I had not heard any since leaving the earth plane. At the entrance was a pair of large ornate gates which were pushed back revealing marble steps that led to the seats. We climbed the steps and found places to sit. Ben declined, saying, 'I have to get back to my work. I hope you have enjoyed your visit.'

We thanked him and asked to visit again. He smiled, gave a wave and was soon out of sight. I turned to Bill and said, 'He seems a nice chap.' 'You're right, Jim,' replied Bill, 'I wonder how long he's been here.' 'I can't answer that,' I said, 'I've been wondering how long we've been here. By not having night, there is nothing with which to measure the days, so I've lost track of time. I will ask Chan when I next see him. I think they're ready to start.'

It was well worth the wait; the music exceeded my expectation. The conductor put every effort into the performance. And even more remarkable was the effect the musicians had on the ether. Wonderful lights formed above the heads of the players, their notes vibrating and creating different-coloured hues. There were blues, pinks and mauves with flashes of gold running through them. The colours danced to the rhythm of the music. The conductor became part of the rhythm. There was a faint blue light around him which at times flashed from his fingertips as he waved his arms. As the music intensified, so did the colour around the conductor. It changed from a light blue to an indigo and extended far from him. It was breathtaking.

As the music became louder, more colours appeared above the players. It was similar to looking through a kaleidoscope, but far more beautiful than anything I'd seen on earth. Each musician was in perfect harmony with the next. At one stage the audience sang with the music. The performance lasted some time until the conductor bowed his appreciation. The lights around the musicians faded rapidly. All that remained was the blue light around the conductor's head and shoulders. The whole atmosphere had become charged and had a tremendous uplifting effect on us. We came away intensely happy and made our way back to the billet.

When we arrived at the billet, we were greeted by the sergeant, who said 'I hope you gentlemen have had an interesting time.' His voice left us in no doubt that he was annoyed with us. 'I've been waiting to tell you that there is a meeting which everyone must attend.' The sergeant was five steps ahead of us as we walked towards the hall. He turned every now and then to tell us how late we were. The meeting was just about to start when we entered and took our seats.

'Good-day, gentlemen,' the captain spoke from the rostrum. 'I've called you together to give you the good news. The war is over, Germany has surrendered.' A loud cheer went up. Many stood up and waved their arms, others sat motionless. Bill turned and gave me an almighty hug which took the breath out of me. I gasped for air and was quite red in the face before I could cry, 'For goodness sake, Bill, you're suffocating me.' 'Sorry Jim,' he said, 'I got carried away.'

The captain called us to order, 'Now, now, gentlemen. The war may be over on the earth plane, and hopefully there will be a decline of young souls coming here. But our work has only just begun. The battle still continues between the forces of good and evil on the lower astral plane. At the moment the battle is going our way, but don't underestimate the enemy.

The evil powers are not yet beaten; they have only shifted their ground. Before long they will break out elsewhere on the earth plane. This will cause great discomfort until people turn away from their destructive, materialistic path. Materialism can only lead to war between brothers and sisters, thereby creating untold hardships for many. Let us hope that something has come from this war. Already it is being called a Great War, but there is nothing great about war. Governments must work together to bring about a better world for tomorrow's children.

'It is peculiar that when evil powers sweep into control, they are never able to make a stable government. Sooner or later they turn upon themselves and collapse into a state of anarchy, which is not a fair democracy, nor does it allow freedom of expression. It takes away liberty and self-will and replaces them with fear which introduces tyranny as the living hell. Those on earth are celebrating the war's end, and we shall too. There will be a get-together later. You will be informed when and where. I'll say goodbye and God bless.'

I felt jubilant about the end of the war. The hall was an uproar of singing and laughter. Bill and I joined in until we felt it was time to head back to the billet. Before entering Bill turned and said, 'I think I'll go for another walk.' 'Would you like me to come with you?' I asked. 'No,' he replied, 'I would like to be on my own.'

I was worried because I felt Bill had come down with a bang. I did not want him to be on his own so I again asked if he would like me to come. He was adamant about being alone. I knew no harm could come to him so I bade him farewell. I had an awful feeling that I might not see him again; but this was silly so I put it out of my mind. When I went inside I was alone because everyone was still celebrating. This wasn't good because I had time to think. I sank into self pity and tried to shake it off, but it came across me in waves. I became irritated with myself and sat down to think of the places that Chan had taken me.

The bathing pool repeatedly popped into my mind. I jumped up from the chair, excited with my decision to return to the pool. Right, I thought, let's try. I closed my eyes, thought of the pool, and firmly held the picture in my mind. I directed my will to the thought and started to pull. A sense of lightness and movement came over me. This time I did not open my eyes.

Splash! I was in the water instead of on the bank. Oh, hell, I thought as I dragged myself out. I got here, but next time I'll concentrate on the bank. I took off my clothes and re-entered the pool. I bobbed up and down for about an hour as I thought about the end of the war. The captain was right. It's human nature for people to find something to fight about. I wondered if they would ever learn. I reached to check if my clothes were dry, and dressed. Just as I finished putting on my shoes, I heard a chuckle from behind a tree.

My curiosity led me to look behind the tree. I might have guessed. Chan with that all-knowing smile on his face was sitting on one of his chairs. My attention was immediately drawn to Chan's feet. Peering through the bottom of his clothing was the most unusual cat I had ever seen. 'What's that?' I asked. 'A cat, of course,' he said. 'Can't you see?' 'I know that,' I said, 'but what kind of cat? I've never seen one like that.' 'He's a Siamese,' he replied. 'His name is Mr. Chow and he's a friend of mine.'

'Surely you mean a *pet*,' I said. 'No, I don't mean a pet,' he replied. 'A friend is what he is. If he were a pet, I could dominate him. Here you can't have dominance over any individual being who has his own willpower. By showing love to Mr. Chow and by giving him freedom, I have remained his friend for years. He always comes to visit me.'

'I have a question,' I said. 'How did you know I was here?' 'Quite simple,' he replied. 'I placed the idea of the pool into your mind. It's my job to take care of you. This means I must know what you are thinking and doing.'

'Well I'll be da . . . ,' I started. 'Don't say it,' barked Chan. 'You were in need of help, and I did not want to intervene directly. The next best thing was to plant a thought. The rest you were able to do. To my mind it worked quite well. I want to congratulate you on your effort; just a slight hiccup. With practice you'll perfect it. Now, for a surprise, we are going to the fifth plane.'

'I thought I could not go there until I was ready?' I queried. 'That is quite right,' he replied. 'You have done extremely well since coming here and have learnt much. Your learning has affected your mental atoms, making them vibrate at a much quicker pace. As this happens, the body also needs to quicken; otherwise the mind soon burns out the body.

'In most cases the body keeps up with the mental attitude. But in your case the learning of truth became fuel for your mind, taking you into states of rapture. Therefore you will soon be ready to evolve on to the next plane. Your current plane is where the wheat is sorted from the chaff. Your ability to learn places you with the wheat. When you evolve on to the next plane, you must realize that your work starts in earnest.

You will put into practice what you have been taught. Our little treat is to show you what it is you are working towards.'

For the first time in my life I was stuck for words. I stood in silence until Chan's cat jumped on his lap. It was obvious the cat had a mind of his own. He seemed to talk to Chan, who appeared to understand. Mr. Chow was the first domestic animal I had come across since leaving the earth plane.

'I sense you have another question concerning animals,' he said. 'By now you are aware that I can read your thoughts, just as I can read Mr. Chow's. Some other time I will explain about the evolutionary line of the animal kingdom.'

Chan put the cat down and rose from his seat. He turned, gave a wave of his hand, and the seat disappeared. I had seen this on several occasions but still found it fascinating. Chan looked to where Mr. Chow was lying and spoke to him. He then turned to me and said, 'Mr. Chow wants to meet you.'

The cat came across to me and sat down, his eyes piercing deep into mine. He then purred and ran back to Chan. 'Are you satisfied now?' asked Chan while patting the cat's head. He then waved his hand, and the cat was gone. I shouted, 'You've not dispersed him, have you?'

'Of course not,' he replied, 'how could you think such a thing after all I have been saying? Mr. Chow is not able to use his will in quite the same way as we can so I assist. We are limited by our conscious development; members of the animal kingdom are also limited by theirs. Each is on his individual road of evolution. You will be surprised to hear that animals are on a rung of the ladder just as we are. Some are far below, others just one rung below. All are climbing to better express the God within. Now if you are ready, we shall go.'

Chan lifted his arm towards me, and I took hold. Right away I sensed his willpower. There was an immediate effect, similar to being in a lift. Within moments we arrived. A brightness hit me like a flash of lightning and blinded me for a few seconds. 'Chan, I can't see,' I shouted. 'Wait a moment,' he replied, 'I will help.'

Once again I sensed Chan's iron will affecting me. It felt as if I were being cocooned in a fine cloth. 'You can open your eyes now,' he said. This time the brightness didn't bother me; however, I found it much harder to breathe. 'This is normal,' he said, 'just relax and take deep breaths occasionally.'

I finally saw that we were on a hill overlooking a valley. It was absolutely breathtaking! Rolling hills were carpeted in emerald green; each plant blended with the next. The whole shone with a lustre more like a never-ending sea than a valley filled with woods and flowers. Many of the trees were in flower, and the scene stretched as far as the eye could see.

Here and there were small houses, and I asked if people lived in them. 'Yes,' replied Chan, 'they are lovers of nature and feel at home in this environment. There are also towns and villages, just as there are on the earth plane. When you are fully ready for the final transition, this will be your home. Come let us walk, we have the time.'

'Speaking of time,' I said, 'can you tell me how long I've been in my new world? I've lost all track of time. I'm not complaining, of course, because it's nice not to be governed by a clock. In one way I'm enjoying myself, but I still miss my parents.'

'I knew you would ask about this,' he said. 'I have already calculated your time here. You've been here twenty-two earth months, give or take a day.' 'But that's impossible,' I said. 'It seems as if I arrived only last week.'

'Of course, you have lost all sense of time,' he said. 'The reason is that you are vibrating at a much higher rate. Your days are made up of things that give you the most spiritual satisfaction, not the labours of the earth plane which can suck away your internal life force.

'Time as you know it is of no importance to spirit. Time and space are earth's limitation. Wherever you are, you can always be as near to me as you are now. A thought sent in any direction speeds in a flash to its destination. Now, do not look back. Instead think in the living present, not in the past or the future. There is no tomorrow because, when it comes, it is today. Today only is ours. Thoughts of the past fog your mind and create a sense of depression. Do not let such thoughts dim today's light. Now, let us walk on.'

There were pine trees on either side where we walked which filled the nostrils with a heavenly scent. The grass was so beautiful that I hesitated to step on it. We descended into the valley. As we did, I became even more aware of the grass because it was covered with all manner of wild flowers that are only seasonal on the earth. The most striking were wild poppies which were dotted here and there, creating the illusion of miniature suns reflecting in a green sea. Slowly the colours blurred. I knew this meant it was time to leave, but I could not wait to live here permanently. Chan smiled and asked if I was ready to leave. Once again we were on the move and quickly appeared at the same spot by the pool. It was as though we had never left. Only my cherished memory of the visit remained.

'I told you it would be a surprise,' he said. 'Eventually you will live there. Until then, you must work to earn the right to live there. What you have seen is only the icing on the cake, not the cake itself. As one climbs the ladder of progress, the planes become more refined. You have already noticed this on your visit to the fifth plane. Although it may be unconscious, the calling to all souls is to come higher. From now on, let it fill your consciousness. Strive ever towards the call because it's for your benefit as you have seen today.

'We are going to visit the earth plane next. I have some work to do and would like your help. In return you will gain experience. When we have finished, we shall visit your old home.'

4

I was delighted to be given something to do, and the thought of seeing my parents made me even happier. Chan approached and asked, 'Are you ready?' I took his arm, and we soon appeared in a place reminiscent of a battlefield. We walked for some time until we came to a seemingly deserted town. We entered the town square where several people stood talking. Most of these were higher astrals like Chan. 'What's going on?' I asked.

'There has been an intrusion from the second plane,' he said. 'It is only a minor one, but we must turn them back. Otherwise, the trickle will become a flood, and all-out war will be declared. We are here to discuss tactics.'

We walked over to where the others stood. One man seemed to be the spokesman. He was not very big and looked unimportant. Had he not been wearing a monk's cowl, you would not have looked twice at him. He began to speak; and, even from where I was standing, I sensed his willpower.

'My brothers,' he said, 'I am pleased to work with you again. I have called you together because there is work to be done. A dozen or so newly slain are in these ruins. They are held by their lower emotions and fed by evil souls who will use them in the climb out of their own dark hell. You must take care because these dark forces will use every trick to hold on to the new souls. So stay alert at all times.' The monk then paused for a moment before continuing. 'I see we have some new helpers.

I am pleased to welcome you. We need every assistance in these operations. As it is your first time in this work, you will come under my jurisdiction. The rest of you are well versed since we have worked together many times. Before we begin, let us pray.'

'What has Chan got me into,' I wondered. 'It doesn't seem too healthy around here.' Chan patted me on the back and told me to listen to the prayer. It was very inspiring and helped me overcome my fear. The words infused us with the monk's love, charging our batteries for the coming fight.

The group was split into twos, except for the newcomers. When the others had gone, there were four of us left. The monk walked over to us and introduced himself as Brother David. He spoke briefly about his work and how pleased he was to have us with him on this mission.

It was time to go, and David led the way. We soon reached the part of the town held by the lower astrals. The buildings were in a state of decay, and the mist was very thick in places. It reminded me of the earth's smog; you know, here one minute, gone the next. Occasionally I noticed shadowy figures leering at us from the corner of the buildings. We passed through the fog. David still led and projected a light, making it quite easy to follow. With every step I felt a greater strength of purpose.

We soon stopped outside a building that resembled one of the seedy drinking dens on earth. The door was partly damaged, which gave me the opportunity to look in. There were six people inside; some stood at the bar, others sat and played cards. My attention was drawn to one of the darkened corners. An overwhelming sense of evil crept over me. A huge black mass lurked in the shadows. I saw the evil of this mass but felt that the souls we had come to rescue could not. I turned to David and asked, 'What is that?' I think in my heart I already knew.

He pulled me away from the door and said, 'You must take what I am going to tell you very seriously. The four souls we are here to rescue are being encouraged to debase themselves by two lower astrals. The evil one lurking in the corner draws on the negative energy to increase his power. When we enter, you must stay close by me. Do not leave my side for any reason. I didn't expect the evil one to be so close.'

There was very little time to be afraid because with one push of the door we were inside. The pungent smell of decaying flesh filled my lungs; a feeling of nausea swept over me. I wanted to run away as fast as I could, but I knew that I could not. We went directly to the souls who were in need of help. They looked around with surprise to see the five of us standing here. 'What do you want here?' shouted one of the lower astrals.

I looked towards the corner and saw the evil one trying to hide. If he showed himself now, the game would be over. It was up to the two lower astrals to hold us back. They were no match for Brother David. With a wave of his hand and an utterance, they fled. This seemed easy. On seeing what had happened to his minions, the evil one came into the fray. This was a different kettle of fish. He towered above us. What little light we had disappeared.

I looked for the four we had come to help and saw them huddled under a table. I saw the fear in their eyes as they watched the appalling apparition come from the corner. Its face resembled something out of hell. 'God!' I thought, 'help.' The evil one must have read my thoughts. Its hideous mouth opened and spoke in a slurred manner; an obnoxious smell oozed from every word. It became unbearable to breathe as these words rolled from the evil one's filthy lips. 'God! Damnation is yours. All that is mine, is mine; and I claim these souls as mine.'

Brother David immediately turned to us and commanded, 'Think only of the light and don't be distracted from it. The evil one is trying to frighten you so he can feed on it for strength.'

David then turned his attention to the evil one: 'In the name of the Most High, he who has cast you into the pit of your own desires, I claim these souls in his love. And by my will, I command you to go.'

I realized the battle was an intense struggle of wills between the forces of light and darkness. I concentrated on the light, and an immense surge of energy flowed through me. On seeing my three friends, I knew they too were experiencing this new-found surge of energy.

The battle was equal. Neither gained ground until Chan and another astral entered the room. On seeing what was happening, they joined the fight. Their added willpower defeated the hideous thing, and it started to lose ground. 'Curse you, curse you,' it snorted as it disappeared. 'You have not won, there will be others.' 'I am afraid it is right,' said David. 'There will always be others.'

A shimmer of light entered the room, which made it easier to see. The stench decreased steadily. My immediate concern was with the poor souls we had come to help. I walked over to the table and lifted it from the four who still cowered underneath. They looked pitiful; they were fast sinking into the trap set by the evil one. Their eyes had sunk into the sockets, leaving a gaunt expression on their faces. 'Come, you're safe now,' I encouraged.

When my friends saw what I was doing, they came to help. I reached down and grasped the hand of one of the victims. The hand felt like a cold, wet fish. My immediate reaction was to pull away, but something inside me forbade this. 'Come, you are to follow me,' I commanded. We gathered the four of them and headed towards the town square.

As we walked along, I thought about these poor souls and the scene we had just witnessed. How lucky I was to have been found by the captain and not to have ended in this place. We were the last to approach the town square where Brother David waited. The other groups had also been successful. We led our group into a square that had been formed by the other rescuers. Chan told us to stand guard.

I was sure they had no willpower left. The fight had knocked it from them. David entered the square and spoke: 'Now listen, we have come to help you escape from the evil that stalks souls such as yours. Some of you have already seen the evil that awaits you here. You are on a slippery path, my friends, one which will eventually lead you into hell. Mend your ways, or you will end up there. Do not turn your backs on this chance. You will not get another. If our help is not wanted, you may go with God's blessing.'

Two of the higher astrals stepped to one side. Only three who were held in the square came forward and moved quickly out of sight. The rest argued among themselves. The four we had helped convincingly described what they had witnessed.

After much discussion, one of them stepped forward and spoke hesitantly: 'We would like to come with you.' Tears rolled down his bony features. 'Please help, I don't want to go back to that nightmare.'

He fell on his knees and cried like a child. My heart went out to him because I felt he was deeply ashamed. Brother David bent down, took hold of his arm and helped him up. For several minutes he spoke to him in a voice full of compassion. Brother David then turned to the others and spoke to them as well. Everyone present felt his love and compassion as he spoke: 'I am glad you have come to your senses. We shall now take you to a place where you will be helped.'

I sighed a silent 'thank you' to God for being with us. Brother David turned to us, the helpers, and asked us to join hands, forming a chain around the souls in the middle of the square. He then raised his hand and made a gesture in the air. A light formed immediately above his head and spread over all of us.

Cries rose from those inside our chain. But the cries died down as the light faded revealing a hospital. We led them into the building and were met by a sister and some nurses. We were told to wait while Brother David spoke at some length with the hospital staff. The nurses then led away those we had brought with us. Before the last one turned the corner, he stopped and smiled, as though to say thanks. This was the last time I saw them.

I made my way over to Brother David and asked, 'What will happen to them now?' 'They will be looked after,' he replied, 'until they are ready for education into the higher life.'

'If we cannot die again,' I questioned, 'why have we brought them to a hospital?' 'A logical question,' he replied. 'You are quite right, we cannot die a second time. The experiences we have in life leave an impression on the unconscious mind. These impressions become reality here because our minds inflict the measure of our thoughts on to us. We are either sent into heights of rapture or into the pits of our own desires. The souls we just saved were in this type of pit. Their weak wills made them easy prey.'

'We are not concerned with their bodies; their minds need healing. In this hospital they will be given rest, taught to overcome their negative thoughts and to face their responsibilities. Eventually they will make good citizens.'

'We'd just finished our conversation when the sister reappeared and spoke to Brother David. We then left the hospital and moved on, soon arriving at a stream. The water glistened brightly. The grassy banks looked so inviting that I was more than grateful for a chance to rest when Brother David asked if we cared to sit. He remained standing. When the rest of us were seated, he addressed us on self reliance. 'We cannot walk another's path for him. Each individual must take every step of it himself. We may hold a guiding light for those whose eyes are open and surround them with spiritual strength. Neither a spirit nor a human being should attempt to control another's mind or to compel him to act against his will. We should be co-workers, helping each other in the Christ spirit. We can inspire, aid and guide, but never compel.

'It is not right to say you do not trust your own strength, because that is what you must trust. The spirit permeates you individually—you are it. It is your spirit, and it is strong enough to rule your mind and every cell of your body. By not trusting it, you disown it. Any thought of doubt, any word of fear must be extinguished before it takes form or expression. Believe in your God within, and all power is yours.'

'What a wonderful address,' I thought. It took away any possible fear I had about my new work. Brother David thanked the higher astrals. He turned his attention to us. 'Again I thank you for your help. Today each of you has shown courage and strength that surpassed our expectations. Your teachers were right to have put you forward for this work. I hope we will work together again; until then God bless you.'

Brother David made the sign of the cross, then started to shimmer and fade. His words still echoed in my ears. When he had gone, Chan came across to me and held out his hand. I took hold, and he pulled me to my feet. Not a word passed between us because no words were necessary. This was the first time I understood the full meaning of Chan's teachings. Chan broke the silence by saying 'You have lived up to my expectations.'

My thoughts flashed back to the time when Chan had spoken to me about the lower planes and how he thought I could work there with him. 'He had it all worked out, the crafty so-and-so,' I thought.

'Now, Jim, I can read your thoughts,' he said with a smile. 'I promised to take you to see your parents after our work was over, but any more strain would be too much just now. Instead I suggest we go to the pool so that you can wash off the stench of the battle.

Chan held my arm, and again we were away. We re-appeared by the pool. The water shimmered before my eyes, inviting me to enter. I wasted very little time undressing and in so doing disturbed the pattern on the water formed by some overhanging branches. Chan declined the invitation to join me and sat under one of the trees.

For some time I soaked up the energy which the water gave freely. I was pleased with the way I had conducted myself in the fight and felt lucky to have Chan as my teacher. I felt much better now and decided to dress. I walked to where I had laid my clothes and was astonished to find them gone. In their place, a handsome robe of many colours was neatly laid out. This must be Chan's doing, I thought, and turned towards the tree where he was sitting. 'What's all this about then?' I shouted and picked up the robe.

'Put it on,' he replied, 'that's a good fellow. We do not want people talking about you.' I looked down at myself, flushed with embarrassment, and quickly put on the robe. It fitted beautifully and felt extremely comfortable over my shoulders. There was also a pair of funny-looking shoes which I slipped on. If my friends could only see me now, they would think I was going to a fancy dress party. Chan beckoned me to sit next to him.

I walked carefully to the chair he had materialized. I had to walk carefully in the new shoes; otherwise, I would have fallen over. Even though I was dead, I still felt pain as I had not yet learnt to control that side of my mind. I stood in front of Chan and asked, 'What do you think?'

'You look exquisite,' he said, 'just like an emperor from my period. Now come and sit down. I will explain why I have changed your clothes.'

When I had made myself comfortable, Chan continued:

'The most important part of my teachings so far has been the creative principle of thought. You know, from your experience in the recent battle, that thoughts—good or ill—can be reflected back on to oneself. This has happened to you. Your emotional thoughts induced by the conflict of battle have affected your mental aura.

'It will be necessary to cleanse your emotional field every time you work in this way. As yet I have not taught you how to do this, but I did the next best thing by suggesting you bathe. In this way the magnetic force of the water has automatically cleansed not only your body, but your magnetic aura as well. As your thoughts gathered momentum in battle, they not only affected your mental aura but also your bodily one. All that your body has contacted, such as your clothes, has held on to your vibrations either good or ill. It will be necessary to cleanse not only the mental aura but your clothes as well. If you think back to the first time you bathed here, you will remember you also put on new clothes.'

'Oh yes, I remember,' I said, 'you took away my uniform.'

'That is quite correct,' he replied. 'I explained why at the time. This time I took it upon myself to give you new ones. The clothes I have furnished are a present from me. I do not expect you to wear them all the time. When we leave, I will materialize western clothes for you.

'I must apologise to you. You were to attend an armistice party; instead I got permission for you to work with me. It will not be long before you move out of your billet because your adjustment period is nearly over. You have earned the right to move to a higher plane. This explains why we visited the fifth plane. I also needed an opportunity to introduce you to the work for which we thought you were most suited. There are souls who would like to work with us in these operations, but they do not have the right mental outlook and lack the necessary willpower. You possess these two necessary qualities as you have already demonstrated. The rest I am working on.

'Now let me explain something about the aura to you. You have noticed that you cannot lie here because your whole life can be read by someone capable of reading another's pattern-of-life. Yours was read when you first came here. It indicated your strengths, weaknesses and ideas.

'From this assessment, we were able to determine the correct path upon which you should walk. I was approached by those who thought I would make the most suitable teacher, and I gladly accepted the opportunity to help.

'Everyone has a pattern-of-life. It is an imprint of every thought and emotion the soul has experienced, not only in one lifetime, but many. Some would argue it is the blueprint of the character, others would refer to it as the Akashic records. Both would be right.

'I like to think of it as the Book of Judgement because that is exactly what it is, our own book of life. We the authors write a play within the book, and we the players put on the correct mask to suit every experience throughout each lifetime. This is why the Law of God is perfect, because he allows us to be our own judges, jurors and executioners. We cannot escape from ourselves because we are the Law made manifest.

'I would like you to think back to when we first met. I took you for new clothes and on to the pool where you bathed. I spoke about the cars on earth requiring a battery. We compared them with astral bodies and said both utilized batteries for motion.' Chan had a wonderful memory. It took me a while to think back to that period of my life, but with Chan's prompting I recalled the lesson.

'Good, you do remember,' he said. 'The physical body also requires a battery. In each case the battery not only holds a charge but also leaks a charge into the ether which creates a magnetic field around the vehicle. This field of radiation is called the aura. The human and astral auras are much more complex than others because they are always in a state of constant flux. At times the aura can be seen around the human body as a cloud of electrons that shimmers from head to foot. Its density increases and decreases with the mood of the individual. Jim, I know these words are new to you. In time you will be taught their meaning and significance.

'Every material thing on the earth has a field of radiation around it, but man has the most complicated. By acting on the mental atoms, his conscious thought creates a pattern within the field. This is the part of the aura seen by those on the earth who have developed their sixth sense. However there are two other more refined vibrations. They are the mental and the spiritual. Both are affected by the finer ethers and, of course, are affected by the person's mentality.

'Within these fields large pulsating colours change from moment to moment. From his birth into the physical world, man builds his character. The sentient atoms pulsate with his thoughts and are the bricks and mortar of his structure:

'The tones and consequently the colours of the human aura are irrefutable manifestations of what the self makes or moulds from the opportunities in his earth life. They indicate his physical, mental and spiritual states. Thus the tone and colour of the aura reflect the man himself.'

Chan's talk was interesting, so I asked if he would explain more about the colours of the human aura. 'There are seven major colours which form the aura,' he said. 'Each has its own vibration, and each is influenced by the thinker. I will give an example. You have heard of someone seeing red after an outburst of anger. If you look at his aura immediately afterwards, you will notice large pulsing shades of fiery red which reflect his mood. This is the first colour of the human constitution. What are the other six major colours ... Jim?'

Chan caught me on the hop because I could not remember what I had been taught at school about colours. 'Never mind,' he said, 'I will remind you.' We were there for some time while Chan explained the rest of the colours. He asked me to repeat the sequence of the colours so I would not forget them. 'Red, orange, yellow, green, blue, indigo and violet,' I said smilingly.

'Very good,' he replied, 'they are the seven major colours, but I must explain that there are seven subdivisions of each. The possible combinations of colour hues that make up the aura are countless. You may have noticed from what I have said, there is a threefold aura which relates to the threefold human constitution. These three parts are the physical body, the soul, and the spirit. The physical body is connected more to the etheric vibrations, the soul expresses more on the astral (mental), and the spirit more on the higher mental (spiritual). You must keep in mind that while someone may hide his thoughts from those on earth, it is impossible to lie and cheat here because one's thoughts determine which plane one goes to after physical death. Like will attract like. There is an appropriate saying that you might have heard: As you think, so you become. These words have a great meaning in life. Are there any questions you would like to ask?' I answered that I had none. 'Good, now I will show you how to clean your aura without taking a bath.' I jumped up from the chair and asked, 'Does this mean I will not be able to swim in the pool?'

'Of course not,' he replied. 'Cleansing the aura by thought is necessary, whereas swimming is a recreation. It is a foregone conclusion that thought is quicker than swimming about flapping your arms.' Chan saw the funny side of what he had said, and we burst out laughing. When we had finished, he continued to tell me about cleansing my aura.

'Now that you are standing,' he said, 'we can start. It would be best to close your eyes, then hold your hands out, palms upwards. Now think of a white light entering your forehead and flowing through your body, then bring it out through the palms of your hands. You must use your willpower to operate your thought. Now try it.'

I tried several times before I felt the full force of the energy flowing through me. It had quite an unusual effect. I became very light-headed and was left in a rather heightened mood. When I commented upon it, Chan replied, 'The feeling you are now experiencing is due to your cleansing the aura of all negative thoughts. It is a good indication. Any new feeling of negativity must be cleansed so that you always feel as you do now. It only takes a moment, and of course willpower.'

Chan stopped talking, and sat there with a smile on his face. 'Are you alright?' I asked. Chan took his time in answering. 'I was just reflecting back to when I first came here, so long ago now. I had to adjust in much the same way as you, but I was much older when I said farewell to my family and friends. Yes, Jim, your thoughts wonder how old I am. Would you care to guess?'

I didn't know what to say in order not to insult him. I proceeded carefully. 'At a glance I would say you have been over for two hundred years or so.' I waited for his reaction. 'My boy,' Chan said smilingly, 'you are being too kind.' I made a weak apology for any indiscretion: 'Oh, I forgot you can read my thoughts.'

'I assure you, no apology is necessary,' he said. 'I am over eight hundred and sixteen, yet every day is like a new page for me to write on.' I stood there with my mouth open. I could not believe his age. Chan stood up from the chair, looked me straight in the eyes and said, 'Remember my saying that as you think, so you become? My way of thinking is reflected in my appearance. Your thinking will also reflect in yours, given time.'

Again Chan laughed. I didn't understand his little joke, but after all, I thought, he is a Chinaman with a funny sense of humour. Chan turned, faced the chairs, waved his hand, and the chairs vanished. 'Will you teach me how to do that?' I asked. I expected him to say that he would at a later date. Instead he turned and replied, 'There's no time like the present. The most important thing to remember, when materializing an object, is to hold on to the mental image. Now think of something small to start with. Hold the thought until you are sure you have the correct proportions. Then use your willpower to direct the subjective form into your objective world. Presto, you will have become a magician! Now let me see what you can do.'

I thought it would be best to materialize something familiar, such as one of the books I had had on earth. The one which immediately sprang to mind was *The Adventures of Toby*. I often read it, even though it was for much younger people. I pictured the book's cover and its size, which was only four by eight inches. This part was easy. It was harder to bring the book forward from my imagination, but I was determined. I think I tried too hard because something happened, but not in the way I wanted. A book appeared, but it was much too large. In fact, it barely resembled the book I had in mind. It was the wrong colour and the title read backwards. 'Oh dear, what went wrong?' I asked.

'You have done extremely well for your first attempt,' said Chan. 'Now I will tell you where you went wrong. You had a positive hold on the image of the book, which was good. Your willpower was nicely under your influence, but your imagination ran away with you. You must gain more self control and patience. Now dismiss what you have created.'

'How do I do that?' I asked. 'Simply by looking at the book and dismissing it into the elements from which it was created. More willpower is needed,' replied Chan.

'Right, here goes,' I said. My willpower increased as I concentrated on the book. Within moments the book shimmered and faded. A few moments later it was gone. 'Well I seem to have done alright.'

'Good,' cried Chan, 'now start again. Only take it slowly and bring your imagination under control. You show a flair for this; however it needs working on.'

We were there for quite some time. Finally I held a book identical to the one I had on earth. I smiled at Chan, 'This brings back memories.' Chan nodded. He had the patience of a saint to put up with me, and I thanked him for it. I felt very happy with myself. At last I had achieved something that would benefit me in my new life. I was like a child with a new toy. If I'd had my way, I would have spent the next week materializing anything and everything for the fun of it; but Chan had other plans. He materialized new clothes for me which I hastily put on. The clothes were a present, so I could not tell him they were unsuitable. Later they became some of my most cherished possessions. I noticed a look in Chan's eyes that told me he had a surprise. He started to laugh. 'You are learning to read me. You are quite right, I do have a little surprise for you. We are going to visit your parents. Only this time you will travel by your own willpower.'

5

Oh dear, I thought. I remembered the time I tried this on my own. 'Don't worry, Jim,' remarked Chan, 'I will be close by. Just remember to concentrate on the room in which you wish to materialize.' I was excited at the thought of seeing my parents, and quickly built a picture of the living room that I knew so well. I linked my will to my thought and pulled. The movement began and ended quickly. I opened my eyes to complete darkness. To my horror, I realized I could not move so yelled for Chan's help. His distant voice found me, 'Don't panic, you are quite safe. Just take two steps forward.'

I did as I was told and stepped forward into my parents' living room. Chan stood there smiling. 'What went wrong?' I asked. 'Turn around and look for yourself,' he replied. I did, and faced a wall. 'I don't understand,' I said. 'One minute I'm in darkness, the next I'm facing you.' Chan asked, 'Do you not realize what happened?'

'I'm afraid I don't,' I replied. 'Well, you materialized in that wall,' he said. 'Nothing drastic would have happened, but your arrival there brought more matter to the brickwork than it needs. A little more explanation is necessary. You know your body is not made of the same atoms as the brick. Your atoms are finer and contain more ether, which allows them to pass through the coarser atoms and ether of the brick. Problems will only arise if you linger in the exact spot instead of passing quickly through. Your atoms would then expand those of the bricks and create too much force in too small a space. The loud cracks and noises produced by this excess force are called a manifestation. It is often heard when a spirit visits people on earth.'

'Oh yes,' I said, 'this was talked about in a lesson with the teaching guide. But I was still surprised to find myself in darkness.'

'You must focus your thoughts more clearly,' he said, 'otherwise you will face the same problem on other visits. Now you have first-hand experience of entering a wall. This rarely happens, and now you can easily rectify the situation. Let us find your parents.'

Chan walked towards the wall and went straight through. I hesitated to follow and stood there. He returned and asked, 'Well, what are you waiting for?' I laughed to see him walk through the wall. 'I know why you are laughing,' he said, 'but I do not look as silly as someone I could mention who got stuck there a few minutes ago.'

'You're right. I'm sorry,' I replied and made my way through the wall into the garden. I felt a momentary heaviness as I passed through the wall. Mum sat in her garden chair surrounded by flowers. She only spent time in the garden when it was hot so I deduced it was summer. Observing people's activities and surroundings is the only way a spirit can determine earth's season or time. On our side of life there is no day or night, no clock to watch.

There was a light mist around my mother but, when I walked over to her, I could just make out her features: a little older and greyer, but still my old Mum. I looked around for Dad, but he was nowhere to be seen. I hoped he was home.

'Yes, he is,' Chan answered, 'look towards the potting shed.' I had forgotten Chan was with me. 'This is your treat,' he replied. 'I will stand in the background for now.'

I hurried towards the potting shed. Just before I reached it, the door opened, and Dad stepped out with some potted flowers in his hands. He was a very keen gardener and won many exhibition prizes for his chrysanthemums. He approached within inches of me. I didn't try to touch him but shouted, 'Dad, Dad!' He must have heard me because he looked towards my mother, thinking she had called him. But she was asleep. Dad muttered under his breath, 'I could have sworn I heard Jim's voice. Can't be, he has been gone for three years—such a waste of a young life, such a waste. It must have been the wind in the trees.'

Three years, Dad had said, where had it gone? It seemed like last week that I was in the battle going over the top for my country, arriving in the next world instead of back home with my parents. Tears formed in my eyes.

'One day you will be able to talk to them again Jim.' I knew who was talking to me and turned to reply, 'You always appear when I'm a little down, Chan. I know you're right, and I look forward to the day my family is reunited.' I felt better. 'Good,' he replied. 'Now we must go back to your billet. I have other work to do.'

We reappeared just outside the billet. I talked with Chan for a few minutes, then he left. On entering I found several chaps standing and talking. One stepped forward and said, 'We thought we would take a walk in the park. Would you care to join us?'

'No, thank you,' I replied, 'I need to lie down.' I went over to my bed. Truthfully I didn't feel tired, but I needed to go over Chan's teachings.

Over the next two years I regularly visited the earth plane to see my parents and watched them grow old gracefully together. By this time I had grown both mentally and spiritually and could go on my own without getting into trouble.

I grew to love Chan as my own father. He was always just one step behind me in my earlier years. The time was fast approaching for me to move to the fifth plane. I spent as much time, if not more, on that plane than I did at the billet. If I were to be honest, which of course I am, I did not like going to the billet.

Then something happened to me which I had never experienced before. I was sitting on my bed when I felt a tingling start in my feet that worked itself up my legs until my whole body vibrated. I didn't know what was happening so called for Chan's help. As I waited, my thoughts tumbled over the last two years. There had been a lot for me to learn. We had also had the last lesson from the teaching guide. He told us how pleased he was that we had made such a lot of headway. Now he could hand us over completely to our own guides. But Bill, poor old Bill, was moved to another part of the astral plane. I was told he had difficulty in adjusting, and it was thought best to move him away from his old conditions. For the time being I lost contact with him, but I knew I would meet him again. 'Hmm, Chan is taking his time,' I thought. He must be busy. I spoke too soon because he immediately appeared within two feet of me. 'Ah, there you are,' I said, 'something strange is happening to me.'

'I know,' he replied with a smile, 'it is time for you to leave here for good. You have earned the right to move to your new home on the fifth plane. The feelings you are now experiencing mean that your body is ready to fall away. Just as a butterfly struggles free from its chrysalis to a new world, you too will break free to a higher plane.'

I wondered what would happen next, but I did so with a mixture of fear and happiness. Chan must have read my thoughts and said, 'Now calm down, you have nothing to fear. I will help you. I am as happy as you are that this time has come. You have done extremely well to evolve so quickly to the next stage. I want you to sit passively. I am going to add my willpower to yours, and it will help. Now close your eyes and do not open them for any reason until I tell you. Do you understand?'

'Yes, Chan,' I replied. My mind buzzed with excitement, but I knew I must calm down and relax. I took deep breaths and controlled my feelings. Slowly I felt Chan's willpower converge with mine. The tingling increased until my whole body shook violently. It felt as though I was shaking myself free from a suit of very tight-fitting clothes. Slowly the shaking subsided and was replaced by a sense of lightness. My body was now completely still. 'You can open your eyes now,' he said. I felt hesitant to open them when I remembered the blinding light of my first visit. Chan read my thoughts. 'Now come on, Jim' he said. 'I told you it would be alright to open your eyes. Now that you are an inhabitant of this plane, you will not experience an adverse effect.'

Slowly I opened my eyes to discover that I was sitting in a room that looked very familiar, yet I had not been to this room before. 'Where are we?' I asked. 'You are in your new home,'

Chan replied. 'No more billet, everything here belongs to you. I have been working on this surprise for some time. The furniture and the paintings are what you have appreciated in the past.'

'So that's why it all seems so familiar,' I said. 'But of course,' he replied, 'how else could I have known what you liked? It was easier to read your thoughts than to guess your preferences. I did not build the house myself; there were others who helped. Over a period of time the builders and I brought this house into being for you. The hardest part was finding the right location, but you indicated this on one of your visits.'

'It must have taken some time to build,' I remarked. 'On the contrary,' he said, 'as soon as we knew you were ready to come, we began our work. I designed the house and drew a rough plan for the architect who then, with the help of the builders, created the house. All in all it took a little over a week. The furnishings were left to me.

'But where are we?' I asked. 'Do you remember your first visit to this plane?' he asked. 'Yes, I do,' I replied. 'We visited a valley. I said how beautiful it was, and how I wished I could live there. Wait a minute, you don't mean!' Chan did not give me time to finish before he interrupted: 'Yes, this is where your home is,' he said. 'I hope you like my present. You have worked hard, and this new home is the fruit of your labours. Now come outside, I have something else to show you.'

I lifted myself from the chair and headed towards the door. Before opening it, I turned and had another look at the room. I seemed to recognize every piece of furniture. It was as if each piece reached out to me, yet I had never laid eyes on any of it before. It was a strange feeling, but I was very pleased.

I turned and opened the door. Immediately a loud cheer went up from a group of people standing on the lawn. I turned to Chan and asked, 'Who are they?'

'Your neighbours,' he replied. 'Do you remember the houses in the valley? These people live in them and have come to welcome you. It is customary here to get to know your neighbours. It is the correct behaviour. I will leave you to get to know your new friends. After you are settled in there will be work for you.' Chan stepped to one side and within moments he was gone.

One of the group stepped forward and introduced herself. 'My name is Rose,' she said as she smiled, and held out her hand. I took hold and felt warmth radiating from it. 'You have very soothing hands,' I said. I looked into her deep blue eyes and was so captivated by her loveliness that I stood rooted to the spot.

'What is the matter?' she asked. 'Oh, forgive me for staring,' I mumbled. 'It's been a long time since I have spoken to a woman. I had begun to think men and women were to be kept separate for ever. I was told it was to give our lower passions time to subside, but I don't have any problems in that direction.' We both saw the funny side of what I'd said and laughed.

'What's your name?' she asked. 'James Legget,' I replied, 'but my friends call me Jim.'

'Well, Jim,' she said, 'come and meet the others.' There were five other women and twelve men. Rose introduced me to each, after which we sat in the garden of my new house. It was a glorious day and I felt at home for the first time since coming to this side of life. I had a drink made from wild fruits. It tasted like nectar. My appreciation of this was heightened because

Chan made sure that I overcame my craving for meat. My tastebuds were refined to the process. I found it difficult at first, but now that I understand more about animals I don't see how I could ever have eaten them.

We talked for many hours until finally everyone had left except Rose. 'When you have settled in you must visit me. I live just down the lane from you,' Rose said, pointing in the direction of her house. She turned back to me, placed her hands on my shoulders to kiss me on the forehead, and said, 'Goodbye. Don't forget to visit.' She walked down the path and turned once to wave, then was out of sight. I was very pleased to have such a kind neighbour.

I went inside to examine Chan's wonderful gift. My first impression was that the rooms were small but adequate. There were four rooms in all. The largest was for entertaining. There was a smaller adjacent room with no furniture. The floors were carpeted in a deep blue, and the walls were painted the same colour. 'I know what this room is for,' I said aloud. Chan always made sure that I meditated, so he had incorporated this room for that purpose. A bathroom and a fully furnished bedroom were upstairs. Although we have no need of sleep, it's very hard to break the habit. At times it's nice just to lie down and relax.

My belongings were neatly laid out on the bed: clothes to one side, books to the other. Chan had thought of everything, even down to my belongings. I spent a while putting away my things before taking an exploratory walk. When I reached the bottom of the garden and turned to look at the house, I felt a lump in my throat. Tears rolled down my cheeks. I quickly wiped them away. My very own home, after all this time.

The house was set amongst a group of trees; the garden extended some forty feet from the house. It was alive with the most exquisite flowers one could imagine. The air was laden with the scent of honeysuckle. The only scene I ever saw on earth which compared with it was on a holiday postcard of Devon sent by my aunt Kate.

I walked along the path that I knew would take me past Rose's house—just to see what it looked like and hopefully to see her again. I walked about half a mile before I came to a small pink cottage set back from the path. 'This must be it,' I thought, but she had not said it was a cottage. At first I was hesitant to approach in case I had the wrong cottage, but I walked to the front door where a sign announced, 'Rose's Cottage'. I chuckled at the thought of 'Jim's Place' for my house.

I knocked and waited, but there was no answer. I came away rather disappointed. I made my way further along the path, over a meadow, and across some fields. It seemed I had walked for miles so I looked around for a suitable place to rest. To my left were large oak trees with anemones and bluebells nestled beneath them. Their petals, fully open to the heavens, added glorious splashes of colour to the rich green grass. It was as if they invited me to sit amongst them, but my fear of squashing them prevented me.

I approached one of the trees and sat down with my back against its large trunk. I relaxed and thought how nice it was to close my eyes for five minutes.

Suddenly a cold shiver passed through me, and I felt someone touch me. I jumped to my feet and looked around to see if anyone was having a game with me, but I was alone. I wondered from where the touch had come. Again, I felt an encroachment on my aura. As this had first occurred when I sat against the tree, I nervously walked around it. 'I wonder . . .' I said out loud as I thought of the gardener on the fourth plane who spoke to trees and who said he understood them.

Perhaps the tree was trying to communicate with me. I placed my hands on its trunk. The shivering intensified the more I concentrated. I assumed I was having an effect; nevertheless, I was extremely shocked when I felt a strong emotion from the tree. I quickly took my hands from the tree and stepped back. It *was* trying to communicate! I stood there for several minutes with a mixture of fear and apprehension. My curiosity finally got the better of me, and I placed my hands back on to the tree. Again a shiver passed through me. This time I did not pull away. Slowly my sensitivity merged with the tree. I became aware of its totality, from the very depths of its roots to the tips of its branches. Its past experiences passed before me as though I were watching a newsreel. What a wonderful way to understand history. When Ben talked of communicating with the tree, I had not fully recognized or appreciated the immensity of nature, nor that all things in God's garden had such sensitivity. In my enlightened state I became aware of the other neighbouring trees and realized in some mysterious way that the tree I was communicating with could also communicate with its own species. Thus, what one tree sensed, all of them sensed. By my becoming a part of their sensitivity, I would impart a vibration of love. This is what Ben meant when he said, 'By giving them my love, they respond to that love, and grow accordingly.'

I spent the best part of the day thoroughly enjoying learning from the tree. On leaving I thanked the tree, although I thought this might appear odd. But I knew it would respond. I thought about the trees and plants on the earth plane. Mother often spoke of Dad's green fingers. I now knew she was right. Plants responded to his kindness and often won prizes for him at the local flower shows. Dad often talked to his plants. I had thought it was rather silly, but he swore they understood him. How right he was, but I had to die to understand it.

As I passed a hill, I heard the tinkle of falling water. I listened for a moment and made my way towards the sound. I climbed the hill and discovered a small stream that cascaded over some rocks before forming a broad pool in the valley below. Graceful ferns edged the waterfall and the path which led to the valley. I decided to follow the path; but before I did, I stopped to admire the view. Rolling hills were covered in a carpet of emerald green, and large oaks and pines grew side by side on the hillsides.

On descending I was careful not to slip on the grass, which was like silk. I approached the pool and stood at its edge. The water was crystal clear. The only movement on the pool's surface was the shimmering reflection from a ray of light. My attention was drawn to the sides of the pool where large clumps of bulrushes glistened in the sunlight. These created the impression of arrows piercing the tranquillity of the pool. The pool looked very inviting so I decided to have a swim. I looked around to see if anyone was about, but I had the place to myself. I quickly took off my clothes and entered the pool. It was quite deep but I could swim well. I chuckled to myself about my concern with drowning. I came out of the pool feeling refreshed, and was soon on my way to the valley.

I came across a young man and woman and somehow knew they were troubled. I stopped to ask what was wrong. 'It's my father,' the woman replied with tears in her eyes. 'He's a drunkard and wifebeater. My mother is now very ill in hospital, and we are waiting for her to pass over. It's not my mother that I'm worried about. She is a wonderful soul and will come straight here. No, it's my father who will have to pay for what he has done. I love them both, and blame myself somewhat for my father's behaviour. He started drinking heavily soon after I died in a boating accident.'

The young woman suddenly cried uncontrollably. 'I'm sure it will work itself out,' I said. The young man put his arms around the woman and also reassured her. I wondered if I should stay with them, but concluded they would find solace in each other so continued my journey.

I heard singing and moved towards it to discover a large group of people standing in a circle. A man's voice stood out. When I stopped and listened, I realized that the voice belonged to a clergyman. I'm afraid that was not for me. I continued on my way through the valley. Every now and then I stopped to talk with someone; everybody was so friendly.

My next encounter was with a man walking a dog. The dog was not on a lead, but he trotted happily by the side of his owner. 'Well, I'll be a monkey's uncle,' I thought, 'this is the first dog I've seen since leaving the earth plane. Come to think of it, he's only the second animal I have seen. The first was Chan's cat.' My curiosity got the better of me. 'Excuse me, I hope you don't think I'm rude. It's about your dog.'

'What about him?' the man replied, in an abrupt manner. I was hesitant to finish my question for fear of upsetting him.

'I'm sorry, I should not have interrupted you,' I said as I started to walk away.

'Wait a minute,' he called, 'you seem to have a question. I have some spare time, and if you care to sit down, we can talk. By the way, my name's Albert, and this is Ben.' I introduced myself and patted Ben on the head which earned me a lick on the hand. 'Ben seems to like you,' said Albert. 'If Ben thinks you're alright, that's good enough for me.' We found a place to sit, and the dog lay next to us. 'That's better,' Albert remarked as Ben stretched himself out on the grass. 'Now what's your question?'

'Well, Ben is only the second animal I have seen on this side of life. Where are all of them?' I asked. 'To tell the truth,' he said, 'I don't know the answer to this mystery. All I know is that Ben was waiting for me when I passed over. He died just one week before me. We had had a good life together and I missed him very much. You see I never married, and old Ben was wonderful company. When he went, I felt rather lonely. Thoughts about Ben clouded my mind, and I failed to look for traffic when crossing a busy road. I heard the bell of the tram too late. The next thing I remembered was coming to in a hospital bed. I tried to move but was unable to. My mind was alive, but my body would not respond to my commands.

'There was a heavy mist in the room. Occasionally I noticed shadows flitting about in the mist. My hearing had not been affected so I heard what was going on around me. Two of the shadows came forward and bent over me. I gathered they were nurses and that my vision had been damaged in the accident. I heard one of them explain to the other that probably I would not last the night. I thought "How ridiculous I'm sure I will be out of here shortly." How right those words were, but not in the way I expected.

'I drifted off to sleep and had a remarkable dream. I dreamt that my mother and father stood at the bottom of the bed and beckoned me to come with them. It wasn't like any dream I had ever experienced. It seemed so real, but I knew it was only my imagination because my parents had been dead for over twenty years. Seeing them distressed me, and I woke with their images firmly in my mind.

'I could not move my head, but my eyes were able to pierce the mist. I saw my parents' forms standing by the bed. My father stood to one side of my mother, who smiled and said, "Come Albert, it's time for you to leave this place."

'It took every ounce of strength I could muster to raise my head from the pillow and shout, "No, you're dead. You're only a dream." My mother then spoke in a tone that left me in no doubt that she was not imaginary. "Now listen, Albert. You have had a fatal accident. Your father and I have come to take you to your new home."

'Slowly my strength ebbed from me, and I fell back on to the pillow. The two nurses still stood close by, and I heard one of them comment, "He's becoming delirious, it won't be long now." I wanted to sit up and say, "Look, I'm alright," but I didn't have the strength.

'My mind was being pulled apart. On the one hand I had the nurses saying that I was dying, and on the other my parents saying that I must go with them. I screamed, "No more." Suddenly a surge of pain shot through my body shaking me violently, then a feeling of peace swept over me. This was followed by a sensation of floating through a dark tunnel towards a light at the end. The next thing I knew I was standing naked beside the bed. I was startled by my mother's voice, saying "Here, Albert, put this on." She stood beside me with a dressing gown in her hand.

'I doubted the reality of what was happening. I paused for a minute or two and then said, "This is all a dream, you're not really talking to me. I'll wake in a minute." Mother snapped, "I'm no dream. Now put on the dressing gown, that's a good boy." I did as I was told, mostly through embarrassment. The dressing gown felt real enough. "Are you truly my mother?" I asked.

' "Whose mother do you think she is?" said a voice I recognized immediately as my father's. He stepped out of the mist. "Now then, Albert, we have been waiting here for some time. It would be best if you came with us."

'I looked back to the bed and saw a dark shape lying on it. Two distinct voices could be heard coming from the shadowy figures which leaned over the bed. One said, "He's gone poor soul," and the other replied, "It's for the best, he would have been a vegetable had he lived."

'I stood there in disbelief. "Why can't they see me?" I shouted. "It's because you are no longer an inhabitant of their world," said my father. "I don't understand," I quivered and turned towards my mother. "What has happened to me, am I really dead?"

' "I know it's hard to understand," she said. "Yes, in one way, you died five minutes ago in that bed, but only to awaken to a much greater and fuller life. Now Albert, I have a surprise for you." I didn't need any more surprises. Being told that I was dead was quite enough.

'Then suddenly I heard a dog's barking. My thoughts went straight to Ben. I shouted out, "Ben, Ben!" Before I could utter another word, he pounced on me and began licking my face. I fell to my knees and ran my hands over his head. I knew every bump on his graceful old head. It was Ben alright. The joy of seeing him and my parents was too much. I burst into tears. I now was ready to follow them anywhere. They took me to a place to recuperate. It was similar to a convalescent home. My parents visited regularly and brought Ben with them. When I was strong enough, Ben and I were given a small house here.

'I have a neighbour, Miss Carter, who lives just over the hill from me. She has a pet cat and is constantly complaining that Ben chases it, but I am sure they are friends. At times I have seen them lying down side by side. Ben has also been known to lick the cat when he thinks nobody is around. Now you know my life story.'

'Well, that's some story,' I said, 'but what has happened to your parents?' Albert replied, 'I am pleased to say they are very well. They have a small cottage not far from mine. Mother always talked of moving to a cottage in the country when my father retired. But it was not meant for their earth life because they both died in their fifties. My mother died first, then my father followed after six months. The doctors said he died of a broken heart. It was a terrible shock to me because I loved both of them very much. Their house passed to me after my father's death, and I lived there until I came here. The shock had a lasting effect on me, and afterwards I lived a very private life.

'I could not bear to become involved with anyone in case they were taken from me. I suppose this was very selfish, but it was the only way I could live. As the years passed, I became increasingly lonely, so I bought Ben for company. He was the first pet I ever had. From the moment I first saw him, there was a rapport between us. I think his temperament was similar to mine. He was my faithful friend for the last twelve years of my life. I missed him very much when he passed. But, as you see, we are now together. I have never been so happy. Well that's enough of me, now tell me about yourself.'

We spoke at length about how I came to this plane and the problems that arise from one's earth life. Still we did not solve the mystery of the whereabouts of the animals. Time went quickly; and, as much as I would have liked to have continued our conversation, I had other things to do.

I thanked Albert and said I would probably see him again. As I set off for home, I thought what a nice fellow Albert seemed, but perhaps a little lonely. I was pleased he and Ben were reunited. I turned to look back at the two of them and saw the loving affection between them as they lay on the grassy slope.

6

Now I had to decide how to get home—to walk or to think myself there. I had had such a wonderful day that I decided to take the easier way and soon reappeared in my garden. On opening the door, I saw a figure in one of the chairs and immediately recognized Chan. I asked what he was doing. I was very pleased to see him but was a little startled by his presence.

'I dropped in to see how you were coping,' he quickly said. I knew Chan did not do anything out of hand. There had to be a reason for his visit. I was just about to ask, when he interrupted me: 'I am sorry if I startled you.'

'You've been reading my thoughts again,' I replied. 'In a way, I have. You have a question about the animals here. Before you ask how I know, I have been tuning into you periodically throughout the day. I thought, as I have a little spare time, I would show you part of the answer. We will have to visit the earth plane, and what you might see could be distressing. Think about it. When you are ready to make the journey, let me know.'

Chan was a very artful fellow. He knew that my curiosity would be aroused. I said hesitantly, 'There's no time like the present.' He smiled and lifted his arm toward me. I placed my hand lightly on his arm. A few moments passed, and we reappeared in a very misty place. A terrible feeling of fear crept over me as we walked towards a building. It looked like a rundown barn. 'Where are we?' I asked.

'We are standing in front of an abbatoir,' he replied. 'Animals are brought here and forcefully ejected out of their earth bodies long before their rightful time, to provide man's food.' 'So,' I said, 'that's why I sense this fear.' 'Yes, you are sensing the animals' emotions before they die. The whole building has an aura of fear. The animals are tense with fear as they enter. When meat is eaten, it is this fear—not the flesh—that can be harmful. It can create many types of mental and physical problems.'

'I never realized these creatures suffered so,' I said in a rather shameful voice. 'Not many people do,' he replied. 'They have not awakened to the fact that all life is sacred. The animal kingdom has been placed in the hands of man so that he can help it climb to Godhood—not so that he can eat it.'

'Where do all the animal souls go?' I asked. 'I have not seen any animals except a couple of pets.' Chan suggested I follow him, and he would show me. We walked along the side of the building to the back. I stopped. Thirty feet away from where we stood, a vortex of white light came from the ground and rose out of sight. Several people dressed in blue kaftans led the souls of the animals into the light where the animals simply disappeared. I turned to ask Chan what was happening.

'It's a long story, Jim. I can only outline it for you. The animals that are being led into the light are going back to their own group soul. Each animal has gained some experience from its earth life, and these experiences are pooled to help the group soul evolve. When the group soul gains sufficient vibration, it evolves on to the plane of man.'

'You mean these animals don't survive death as we do?' I asked. 'That is quite correct,' he replied. 'Man survives the transition called death, but eventually the animal souls which are led into the light will have the opportunity to walk on two legs. By this I mean they will become conscious of their true identity, but this is a long way off. You must understand, Jim, truthfully nothing can die. It only evolves.'

'So what will happen to the domestic pets I have seen, such as your cat?' I questioned. Chan replied further, 'The pets you have seen on your plane are there through the love and kindness of their masters from the earth plane. For a time they will survive the transition called death. Eventually the call within them will become too great to ignore, and they will be drawn towards their own group soul—with the bonus of human love. Their human companions will have evolved to understand this, and will let them go with blessings.'

'There is much to learn,' I said. 'May I ask just one more question?' 'If you wish,' he replied. 'Who are the people leading the animal souls into the light?' Chan paused for a moment. I sensed he was very proud of the work carried out by these souls. He sighed and then spoke. 'They are the keepers of the light. This task is always performed by very evolved beings who have totally dedicated their lives to it.' 'May I meet them?' I asked. 'No, Jim, not until you have evolved enough to understand their work,' Chan answered.

It was time to journey home. On our arrival Chan stopped and sat with me. We talked over the day's events until he decided I needed to be on my own. I thanked him for giving me a first-hand answer to my question; he then left. Chan and I had a deep friendship by this time, and I looked up to him like a father.

I was exhausted from our trip and needed to relax and

gather my thoughts. I decided my new meditation room was the perfect place. A wonderful sense of peace flooded over me as I sat cross-legged on the floor. The whole room was alive with energy lifting my consciousness to a great height. I was able to communicate with the God force within me and listen to the words of encouragement which flooded into my mind. Listening is the true art of meditation. Many people pray to their God for help and guidance, but they do not bother to listen to his words of encouragement.

We are taught about God's love as soon as we are able to accept the new conditions of life after death. He is not the abstract God that most humans on earth get to know. Here we recognize that God is at the heart of everything; he is the one power that flows through all creation. You can only truly know yourself when you understand that God is the only well from which you can draw the water of life. There is no other source.

When we have this mental concept of God, we are then taught how to draw on his power. However, until then, we are not left on our own in an objective world. It may appear objective to us, but it has been created by the intangible mind of God, with his will flowing through every image of his creation and giving life to all.

We are able, in a finite way, to use the same method in our own constructions. There were no bricklayers or carpenters needed to build my new house. The architect and the souls who brought the elements together built it with their power of concentration. Beyond the earth plane, all building work is carried out by the power of thought.

Over the next few years I used the meditation room of my new home more than any other. My life and friendship with

Rose flourished. We went on many journeys together, exploring and meeting new friends. We had many things in common, such as the arts in which we both took an active part.

7

I grew in understanding towards the plant life and became a keen gardener. It was on one of my days in the garden when I sensed an inner call to visit my mother. I knew by this call that she was sending up a prayer to me. It was different this time because the call became stronger by the minute.

I linked on to her thought, and within moments I stood at the bottom of a bed. But it was not the bed I had so often stood by when she was asleep. The surroundings were totally new to me. I looked around the room and soon realized we were in a hospital. My mother's unconscious call to me made me realize that she was very ill. I was suddenly interrupted by a voice saying, 'Please move, you will be in the way.'

A grey-haired man, who I assumed was a doctor, approached the bed and did something to my mother. 'What's going on?' I asked. 'May I ask who you are?' came his reply. 'That's my mother,' I said, 'she has been calling me.'

'We have been expecting someone,' he said and introduced himself. 'My name is Dr. Forbes. As you can see, your mother is very ill, and she is not expected to last the night. I have done all I can for her. Her spirit is willing, but her body is giving up. The earth doctors have done what they can to make her last hours comfortable. It now remains for us to get things ready here so that when your mother wakes, she will be met by someone she knew and loved. Otherwise, the shock of her passing could have a dramatic effect on her. It will not be long. I'm going to see if we have a bed for her.'

He was soon out of sight. I didn't know if I should laugh with joy or cry at the thought of Mum being with me. While I waited I looked around the ward and talked with other astral visitors who were also waiting for their loved ones. The doors to the ward opened, and my father walked in with two nurses. They stopped by Mum's bed, where the two nurses left Dad on his own. He held Mum's hand which he occasionally patted and said, 'You will be alright, love, I'm here.'

I fought back my tears on seeing Dad in such a distressing situation. I knew Mum would be alright, but I was not too sure about Dad. I wanted to shout out, 'Look, Dad, Mum will be fine. There's no death.' But, of course, he would not have heard me. I waited patiently at the bottom of the bed for my mother's release. I suppose an hour or so went by, when suddenly, Mum let out a groan. Dad jumped to his feet. 'Doctor, Doctor. Come quickly, my wife.'

A nurse and a doctor responded to Dad's call. The doctor examined Mum and turned to Dad. 'I am sorry, Mr. Legget. She has gone.' Dad walked over to the bed and again held Mum's hand. Tears formed and trickled down his cheeks as he looked helplessly on. He was allowed to stay with her for a few minutes before the nurse took him to one side and gave him a cup of tea.

I wondered what to do next, but Dr. Forbes appeared with a nurse and two others. They stood to one side of the bed as if they were waiting for something. Slowly a mist oozed from the lifeless form on the bed. My mother's astral body, completely intact, was now some two feet above the bed. The cord that we had been told about, and the one I was attached to when I died, broke immediately in Mum's case. She was still unaware of what was happening.

Dr. Forbes and his helpers took control by gathering around her and lifting her on to the stretcher they had brought with them. Dr. Forbes turned to me and asked, 'Would you please follow us?' We left the ward and soon entered a room that had been tastefully decorated. They placed Mum on the bed, and the three helpers left. Dr. Forbes asked me to sit while he examined her to determine whether any treatment would be needed.

When he had finished, he spoke briefly to me: 'Your mother is fine, no other treatment is necessary.' We talked at some length. He explained that some patients were kept asleep so their subconscious levels could be worked on. No instruments were used in this clinic because the rooms had wonderful healing auras which were infused continuously by great souls from above.

I too felt the soothing effect; a sense of peace touched every fibre of my being. I could not have told you how it worked, but I learned later. Dr. Forbes than bade me farewell. But before he left, he turned to me and said, 'By the way, I will be sending a nurse to look after your mother until she is strong enough to leave.'

I sat back and made myself comfortable. I wondered how long I would have to wait for Mum to wake. What a surprise for her to see me sitting by her bed. I day-dreamed about all the things we would talk about. A knock on the door made me jump. The door opened halfway, and a man's head appeared from around it: 'May we come in?'

'Please do,' I replied. The door opened fully and revealed a rather smartly dressed man of about forty. Immediately behind him was a fair-haired, young woman dressed in a lemon, flowered dress with white belt and shoes to match. The couple looked familiar to me, but I had never seen them before. I felt I should know them. The man came straight over and held out his hand, 'Nice to see you, Jim. I've been waiting a long time for this moment.'

I took his hand, which had a grip like a vice. He shook my hand until I thought it would drop off. 'You have the advantage,' I said. 'You know my name, but who are you?' 'Well, Jim, this is your grandmother,' he answered as he pointed towards the lady, who was leaning over the bed. 'And I am your grandfather.'

I was dumbfounded by this news. I had never seen my grandparents when I was on earth, nor on this plane. They died before I was born. I asked why they had not made themselves known before. 'It was not possible,' Grandfather said. 'We were advised to leave you alone until you had developed your spiritual mind. I know this is a sad time for your father, but it's a joy for us. We shall have our daughter with us once again, and we knew you would be here.'

'I understand. What happens to Mum now?' I asked. 'We've a home ready for her,' he replied. 'As soon as she has gained strength, we shall take here there.'

The door to the room opened, and in walked the nurse I had seen earlier. She spoke with a sweet voice, 'Please could you wait outside? It will soon be time for Mrs. Legget to regain consciousness. We do not want her to go into a state of shock by seeing you, now do we? It's best if I explain what has happened.'

The nurse ushered us out, and shut the door behind us. We sat on a wooden bench running along one wall of the corridor. We talked and talked, for what seemed like ages. 'I wonder what is taking so long?' I asked. 'Be patient, Jim,' Grandmother coaxed.

'I suppose she's alright,' I thought. 'After all this time a few minutes longer is not going to hurt.' It was one of the longest few minutes I ever endured. Slowly the door to the room opened. The nurse stepped out and said, 'You may go in now, one at a time. Please be easy with her because she is in a state of shock.'

I trembled as I entered and wondered if she would recognize me. Mum looked up at me from beneath the sheets. I stood rooted to the spot and just stared. My heart leapt to my throat. I felt wet on my cheeks and realized that I was crying. I don't know who spoke first, but I ran to her bedside. 'Jim, Jim, is it really you or am I dreaming?' 'No, Mum, it's no dream,' I answered as I bent over the bed and cradled her in my arms. We hugged each other for some time but were totally lost for words. Nothing needed to be said; well, not at this time.

Mum wiped away her tears and made a fuss about how she must look. I comforted her, 'Don't worry about how you look. You're safe now, and that is the most important thing. When you are strong enough, you will be able to leave here.'

After the initial shock of seeing me had faded, I said, 'There is another surprise for you.' I turned towards the door and called out, 'Everything is fine now.' 'Who are you calling, Jim?' Mum asked. Before she could utter another word, the door opened and my grandmother walked in. You should have seen my mother's face; it was a picture. They greeted each other as a mother and daughter would after a long separation. Mum asked if her father was there. 'Yes,' Grandmother said, 'he's waiting outside.' I volunteered to get him. He sat on the bench nervously twiddling his thumbs. He looked up and asked if everything was alright. 'Yes, everything is fine. Mum wants to see you.'

Grandfather stood up, composed himself and adjusted his tie. 'How do I look, Jim?' he asked. 'You'll do fine,' I said, and we entered the room. We had a great reunion talking about old times. Suddenly Mum became silent. We sensed she had gone into shock again. I immediately asked what was troubling her. 'It's your father. What will happen to him? You know that he is lost without me.' She began to cry. I placed my hand on her hand and said, 'I'm afraid he will have to manage until the good Lord decides otherwise. When you feel better, we will take you to see him—just as I was taken to see you and Father.'

She took notice of what I said. Through her tears she asked, 'You visited me? If only I could have seen you, my life would have been so much happier.' 'I'm afraid it's not always possible for people to see us, but sometimes we leave our mark. I called to you on several occasions, but was heard only once.' I then relayed the incident with Dad in the garden. Mum settled down again and said, 'I prayed every night for you.'

'I know. I sensed your loving thoughts, and they helped me in my early days here. They encouraged me to become stronger so that I could visit you regularly. I remember your holiday in Devon. I know it was Devon because I looked over your shoulder when you wrote a postcard to Mrs. Wilson. I also looked around the boarding house where you stayed. It was very clean and tidy. One day I followed you to the beach. I thought Dad looked funny with his hankie on his head and his trousers rolled up as he sat in the deck chair with his face towards the sun. I remember thinking he might burn his ankles. Do you remember, Mum?'

'Only too well,' she replied. 'He was in a bad way with his blistered ankles and gave me hell for a week. The only damage was to his ankles, and they remained a funny mauve colour.' She paused for a moment before asking, 'He will be alright, won't he?'

'Now, Mum, Dad will look after himself. Anyway, Mrs. Wilson next door will make sure of that. She has always been a good neighbour to you, and I am sure she will continue to be one.'

Grandfather tapped me on the shoulder and indicated that the nurse had come in. 'I'm sorry,' she said, 'you will have to leave now. Your mother needs rest. There will be plenty of time later to be together.'

My grandparents bade Mum farewell. 'I will be back as soon as I'm allowed,' I said. I lingered at the door until the nurse pushed me out. I reminded myself that the nurse was right. There would be plenty of time.

'Would you like to come back with us?' enquired Grandfather. 'We would love to show you where we live and where your mother will live. We have been getting it ready for her. We had a pretty good idea of your mother's choice of furniture and decorations. When we knew her time was near, we engaged an architect to design and build the house. Your grandmother also enjoyed making things for the home.' Grandmother interrupted to ask if we ought to be going. 'Yes, dear,' Grandfather answered sheepishly.

Grandmother held out her hand to me. Within moments we stood in their garden. I saw that it had been lovingly created. Every flower was perfect in colour and size. To the left of where I stood, a small well was covered in deep pink roses. A garden bench was placed to one side of the well. A path ran from one end of the garden to the house. The most extraordinary pansies I had ever seen grew along the path. Each had been individually chosen for colour and size. There were also clumps of night-scented stocks beneath the front windows of the house. As there is no night on our plane, I thought my grandparents might have a long wait for the fragrance from their stocks. But physical laws did not apply here. The air was filled with the sweet scent from the wonderful flowers. It was a pleasure to admire the beauty of such a well-balanced garden.

'Do you like our garden?' asked Grandmother. 'I most certainly do. Who is your gardener?' I queried. 'We do not have a gardener,' she replied. 'It is a combined effort between your grandfather and myself. We spend as much time as we can in the garden, after the many other things we both enjoy—such as the arts. The gardening takes second place.'

'As a matter of fact, we are going to a new play written by Shakespeare. We have been to a number of his plays, and I have actually seen him. He's a funny-looking man and does not look a bit as I imagined. He dresses very modestly and has short hair and a tidy beard. When he was first pointed out to me, I was very surprised. I had forgotten that people change and can look like whatever they choose, within reason of course.'

We moved towards the house. It was more like a cottage

than a house, but they insisted on calling it a house so I didn't argue. The walls were tinged with pink and the door and window frames were white. The door was a two-piece stable door; the top opens while the bottom remains shut. Ivy covered one side of the house and part of the roof. Just above the door a name-plate spelt out 'Harmony', which was certainly appropriate.

Grandmother and I idled about the garden while Grandfather went inside. 'Come on in, Jim,' he beckoned. 'Make yourself at home. Would you care for some tea?'

'Tea, did you say? I have not had a cup since coming to this life—plenty of water, but no food except fresh fruit. I don't really miss meat. The first few months were hard, but now I don't even think about it. But a cup of tea, I can't think it would harm me. Yes, please, I would love a cup.'

Grandmother chuckled to herself and then spoke: 'This is the only luxury that we permit ourselves. Happily, it doesn't involve the taking of life. It is the one aspect of our life that has not changed, and we do not wish to change it. You will find, however, that tea does not taste quite the same as it did on earth.'

'Well, here you are,' Grandfather said as he entered with a tray of teas and walked over to a small rectangular table next to the window. 'There you are, Ray,' he said and handed a cup of tea to Grandmother. 'How do you like your tea, Jim?' he asked. 'As it comes,' I replied. 'May I ask you a question, Grandmother?' 'Certainly,' she answered, 'what is it?' 'May I call you Ray instead of Grandmother?' 'Of course,' she said, 'otherwise, I feel old.'

'And you can call me Charlie,' piped up Grandfather as he

handed me my tea. 'I hope you like the tea.' He sat next to Ray. They both stared at me and waited for my reaction to the first mouthful. I took one sip and said, 'You're right. It's not the tea I remember.' I managed to finish it but declined a second cup. 'I said it was an acquired taste,' said Ray and laughed. 'We can't have everything to our liking, now can we? We have got used to it, haven't we, Charlie?'

'Yes,' came his reply. The two of them got on very well considering how long they had been together. I asked Ray what would happen next to Mum and where she would live. 'She will rest a couple of days or so in earth time. After that we hope to bring her here, where we can look after her until she can move into her own house. We will help her to adjust to her new life, as we, yourself and many others had to. It can be quite a shock for those who do not believe there is life after death.'

'Now, Jim, tell us what you have been up to. We have had many reports from your guide telling us how pleased he was with you. You have an ability to learn very quickly. He is hoping that you will be ready shortly to work with him.'

'As soon as I know Mum is well, I will talk with Chan. I have decided to take his advice about the work he thought suited me.' I went on to explain about the encounter I had with the lower astrals on the third plane. Ray said she thought I would make an excellent rescuer, and that I should feel very privileged to have been asked to help.

Time seemed to slip by. 'Oh, well, I'd better make a move,' I said and rose from the chair. Charlie came up to me and shook my hand. 'Now you know where we live,' he said, 'please visit us whenever you wish.' Ray echoed Charlie's words as she gave me a cuddle.

They both stood at the bottom of their garden waving to me. I was soon out of sight of their house and made my way towards where I thought my home lay. I decided to walk part of the way so that I could see this part of the fifth plane. I knew I couldn't get lost because all I had to do was think of the place I wished to be. I covered eight or nine miles taking in the sights, and travelled the rest of the way by thought. Once home, I spent some time in meditation and felt very refreshed.

Even though I knew it would be only two days before Mum could leave the hospital, I decided to visit her. I didn't want to go empty-handed so I picked a bunch of flowers from my garden.

On my arrival at hospital reception I was surprised to see how busy they were. One or two nurses flitted about, but the place was filled with the relatives and friends of those who had just passed over. I asked about my mother and was told it would be fine to see her for a few minutes. Mum was sitting up in bed. As soon as she saw me, her face lit up like a fairground on a busy night. She looked a lot better and the wrinkles around her eyes had gone, which took away the look of despair. I asked her how she was feeling. 'Not too bad. Come and sit next to me, I've got such a lot to talk to you about.'

I made myself comfortable on the side of her bed, and Mum told me what Dr. Forbes had said to her. 'He's a nice man and has said I can leave shortly. But where do I go, and what will I do without your father?'

'Well Mum, there is no need to worry. Everything has been arranged. You will stay with Grandmother and Grandfather—or rather Ray and Charlie. I've been told to call them by their first names. It does seem strange that my grandparents are not much older than I am, but I've learnt that anything can happen here.'

I spoke at great length about my life and what I had learnt. Time rolled quickly past. I noticed that Mum was tired; it was time to leave. I said goodbye and promised to return as soon as she had rested. There could be no sudden startles—such as my dematerializing in front of her—otherwise she could go into a state of shock. Mum would be taught this method of travel at a later date.

On my way out of the hospital, I came across Dr. Forbes. 'Excuse me. Could you please tell me how my mother is doing, and when she will be ready to leave?' 'What is her name?' he enquired. 'Martha Legget,' I replied. 'She came here two days ago.' I felt silly expecting him to remember her. He probably saw dozens of souls a day. 'Let me see,' he said. 'Hmm, I do remember someone of that name. If you would wait at reception, then I will examine your mother, and let you know the results.'

I went to the reception area and made myself comfortable. After a while a nurse called my name. 'Mr. Legget? Ah, there you are. I've been looking for you. I am sorry to have kept you waiting. The doctor is unable to speak to you personally but has asked me to tell you that your mother's progress is very satisfactory. She will be ready to leave tomorrow.'

I thanked the nurse for her help, and brightly left the hospital knowing that all was well. I decided to tell Ray and Charlie the good news; I soon materialized in front of their home.

'Hello Jim!' I turned and saw Charlie sitting on the bench near the well. He had a book in one hand and in the other held a plant which grew in abundance here. He seemed to be comparing the flower with the picture in the book and made some comment about its not being quite the same. 'I'm sorry to disturb you,' I said, 'but I wanted to tell you that Mum will be coming out of hospital tomorrow.'

I was unable to continue. Charlie jumped up from the bench and said, 'We must tell Ray the good news right away. She will want to get things ready.' Charlie called to Ray as we entered the house. A voice from upstairs replied, 'I'm up here, dear.' Charlie went to her while I waited at the bottom of the stairs. I soon heard Ray's voice saying, 'We must make sure that everything is in order.'

'Yes, dear,' Charlie replied. 'Don't worry. I've done everything you asked.' I thought it best to leave them as they had such a lot to sort out. I did not want to be in the way. 'I will call back later,' I said to Charlie, 'and perhaps we can meet Mum together.' He thought this was an excellent idea.

I stepped into the garden and waved goodbye. I reappeared in my own garden. On entering the house I was greeted by a familiar voice: 'Ah, there you are. I've been waiting for you. I hope you do not mind my entering your home like this.'

'Not at all, Chan. You're most welcome at any time. I've not seen you in a long time, and a lot has happened to me. I've met my grandparents, and my mother has come over. As a matter of fact, I've just come from the hospital.'

'Yes, I know,' Chan replied. 'Although I have not been with you in body, I have linked with you by mind. I know exactly what you have been up to and have left you alone so that you could adjust to your new environment. You also needed to be here for your mother's arrival.'

'You knew that my mother was coming here?' I asked. 'Of course,' Chan replied. 'We have everything worked out. There is nothing left to chance. Now to the reason why I have come. It is time for you to consider your new occupation. With your permission I will be sending along some people to discuss the work. You will find them most pleasant. They died in similar circumstances to yourself and have chosen to work with us. They have progressed very quickly here, and their characters are very suitable for this work. I have taken too much of your time and must be going.'

I was left alone to think over his words. It would be good to meet others. I was still a bit wary about the work Chan had in mind, but I knew in my heart it was the correct path for me. I felt I should go into my meditation sanctuary where I could draw on the higher forces. It was all still very new to me, but I was learning quickly. I felt much better afterwards.

Time had flown by; it was time to collect Mum from the hospital. But I had to meet Ray and Charlie, so my first port of call was their home. It only took seconds to materialize at their door. Charlie called for me to come in.

The hall had a refreshing atmosphere. Fresh flowers had been placed there, each chosen for its scent. 'You like Ray's handiwork?' asked Charlie. 'Oh yes,' I said, 'she has been working hard.'

Ray greeted me from the door of the living room. 'This is the big day,' I said. 'Yes,' replied Ray, 'we are very excited. I have your mother's room ready. There are things which she'll recognize so she should feel at home immediately.' Ray turned her attention to Charlie. 'I hope you're not going in your gardening clothes,' she said. Her voice left no doubt as to who wore the trousers in this house.

Without a word Charlie disappeared up the stairs. While we waited for him, Ray and I talked about the fear of dying. 'If people only knew about this world,' I said, 'they would no longer fear death. They would understand it only leads to another stage in their lives.' 'You're right,' remarked Ray. 'But there are those who do believe in this life, and to them death is no longer the "king of terrors". They know their friends await them—to welcome, console and instruct them in the ways and work of this larger life. They realize it too will be a life of progression.'

'Quite right,' said Charlie as he came down the stairs adjusting his tie. 'You never knew your grandmother was a philosopher.' 'No, I did not,' I said. 'Well, she is,' Charlie boasted, 'and a good one at that.' 'Now, Charlie, that's quite enough,' said Ray. 'Jim does not want to hear about my hobbies. Anyway, it's time to be going.'

We quickly arrived in the hospital grounds, which had the most lavishly laid out flowerbeds I'd ever seen. Everything pleased the eye; there was also a light scent that uplifted one. We walked along the path and into the hospital. We soon came to Mum's room. I knocked on the door, and she immediately asked us to come in.

Mum was sitting by her bed, dressed and ready to go. I was lost for words on seeing her smiling face. I cupped her tiny hand into mine and kissed her on the cheek. Ray gave her a little hug. 'I'm glad to see you,' said Mum. 'I've been looking forward to this moment and have been ready for ages. The nurse told me to be patient and reassured me you would be along soon.'

'Well, we are ready to go now,' I said, 'but there is a surprise in the way we travel here.' 'What do you mean?' Mum asked. 'Do we get a tram?' 'No. There are no trams here. All will be explained later. But for now, just take hold of my hand. Oh, I almost forgot to thank the nurse and doctor. I won't be a moment.' I left Ray in charge. I made my way to the reception desk and luckily saw the nurse I wanted. I waited until she finished talking with the receptionist. I then thanked her for looking after Mum and for making her stay a happy one. I asked after the doctor and was told that he was very busy, but that my thanks would be forwarded to him. I felt elated as I re-entered Mum's room.

'Right then, are we ready?' I slipped my hand into Mum's. 'Now, hold tight,' I said. Within moments we stood in front of my grandparents' house. Mum was a little taken aback with this method of travel, to say the least. When she regained her senses, she was amazed to see the beautiful place where her parents lived.

'Oh, Jim, I never thought it would be like this. The garden—how beautiful it is. Your father will be in his element when he comes here.' After her earthly death she still put Dad first. What a woman! The beauty surrounding her took away any fear she had left from her first taste of thought travel. In truth this type of travel can be a little alarming to anyone at first.

'Jim, are there churches here?' Mum asked. 'Yes, Mum. If you wish, you can go to any of them. Many people who come to this side of life still retain their faith and wish to be affiliated to the organization they supported on earth. They draw strength and, of course, companionship from belonging to such organizations. There are many ways and paths that lead to "truth".'

'I don't understand all that,' Mum said. 'But I would like to go to church as soon as possible to give thanks to God for reuniting me with my family.' 'Yes, Mum. As soon as you have settled in, I will take you to a church. I think Ray and Charlie are getting a little impatient. They have everything ready for you.' We made our way into the house, and my mother was shown to her room. Charlie and I talked for some time while Ray stayed upstairs to help her.

'I think they are coming,' I said on hearing the door open. Mum entered the room wearing one of Ray's frocks. Charlie and I stood up simultaneously and said how nice she looked. Ray stepped forward and said that she was taking Mum to get some new clothes. She asked if we would care to come along. I declined the invitation on the grounds that I knew absolutely nothing about women's dresses. 'What about you, Charlie?' Ray asked. 'No thanks, love. I'll give it a miss if you don't mind,' he replied.

I spoke briefly to Mum saying that I would be back later to take her to church. I made my farewells and returned home. I thought how much better Mum looked and knew I need not worry about her with Ray and Charlie to keep her company.

8

I made myself comfortable in one of my armchairs and picked up a book. There was a knock at the door before I looked at the first page. On opening the door I saw two gentlemen. 'Goodday,' the shorter one said. 'We have been sent to talk to you about our working together.' 'Oh, yes, Chan spoke to me about you. Please come in and make yourselves at home.' I offered them some light refreshments before sitting down. 'By the way, my name is Jim.'

'Yes, we know,' again the shorter one spoke. 'This is Harry Willmott, and I'm Jack Purvis. We are both soldiers. Like yourself, we died for King and country. It would be best to introduce ourselves properly. You first, Harry.'

Harry immediately jumped to his feet. 'Number 8/12942 Sergeant H.G. Willmott, A Company, 9th Battalion, 60th Division, 42nd Brigade. Our number is something we never forget, Jim,' he said. 'You have to forgive Harry,' said Jack, 'he still thinks he's in the army. Sit down and get on with it, Harry. We haven't got all day.' I could tell they were good friends, as Harry mumbled something under his breath and sat down.

'Now, where was I?' Harry asked as he composed himself. 'Ah, yes. It was 15th September 1916. I remember it as if it were yesterday. It was an attack from Delville Wood to Flers. Lieutenant-Colonel Morris led the 9th Battalion. We were told to move forward from Fricourt early in the evening to the trenches between Trones and Berefay Woods. This was accomplished without a hitch. Indeed, the only blemish on our careful preparations was the erratic shooting from a battery of 4.2 howitzers which, by some error of ranging, repeatedly fired gas shells into James St. on the left. The 60th Battalion were up in line on the right of the Guards. They had not arrived by 07.20 am. During the halt that followed, the 9th pressed on from behind and caught up with the 7th. They entered the gap trench together. The Coldstream Guards were unable to hold the right flank and keep pace with objectives. This meant that the Rifle Brigade took heavy machine-gun fire from right and rear.

'The leading waves rushed on so closely behind the barrage that they were already waiting in shell holes to dash into their objectives when the barrage lifted and the machine guns opened up. The Companies following up in the rear and the 9th Battalion were severely punished. I was one who met his end that day, but not by a bullet. I slipped and fell head-first into a shell hole. Many were killed in shell holes. Gas lay in the bottom of the holes, and you suffocated if you didn't have a gas mask on. But, as you can see, I'm fine now.'

'That's near on a bloody book, not a quick description of your death,' exclaimed Jack. Harry laughed out loud. He seemed to revel in winding Jack up. He finished by saying, 'Tell him your story now, Jack.'

'I'll put you on a charge one of these days,' shouted Jack. Harry smiled like the Cheshire cat. 'You're right, Harry,' said Jack. They both burst into fits of laughter. I wasn't sure what they were laughing about, but it soon became clear.

'Well,' said Jack, 'I came here a little earlier than Harry. It was 25th September 1915. We were attacking the Bellwarde spur. I was at the head of my men. Oh yes, I forgot to mention that my rank was captain. You can guess the rest. I caught a packet and that was that.' 'Go on, tell him the rest,' said Harry. 'Yes, please continue,' I said.

'Well, if you really want to hear the rest. The latter part of my story revolves around my father. My father was over sixty years old when I died. He had long since retired from an active life on his plantation in the South Seas, and longer still from the Royal Navy. He was unable to bear my loss so proceeded to carry on the work that I had been doing.

'By some expedient that God only knows, this fine old gentleman overcame the strict regulations of the War Office and became a Second Lieutenant in the Rifle Brigade. He somehow contrived to be passed for active service and was posted to my old battalion. Having gone so far it was more or less in the nature of things that he should also be given my platoon. The dispensations of fate were not yet over. On the anniversary of my promotion to the command of "B" Company, the commander who took over was accidentally injured, so my father was given the command of the company that I led nearly a year before. Fate is a strange thing, is it not?'

'It certainly is,' I replied. 'What we have here is a captain, a sergeant and a private. It reminds me of the book *The Three Musketeers*.'

Harry stood up and held out his hand and asked Jack and me to take hold. As soon as we did, his voice echoed from his boots, 'All for one, and one for all.' Well, that did it. We burst into laughter. I quickly realized that Harry was the joker. His strength and courage would see us through the years ahead. Just then a mist appeared, and Chan walked from it.

'I see you are getting acquainted,' he said. 'That's good. You have been brought together for your strengths and not your weaknesses. Each of you has shown that you have the right disposition for the work ahead. Believe me, gentlemen, the work ahead will be hard, so make the most of now.'

Chan stepped back into the mist and was gone, leaving us to discuss the forthcoming work. We could only guess what that work would be, but I was not prepared for the events that would soon enter my life. At the moment, I was happy enough to be given a job. The time quickly slipped by until Jack said he had to leave. 'You're right,' said Harry. 'I suppose we had better go and leave this youngster to his beauty sleep.'

9

I was left to think over our meeting. I decided to spend some time in my meditation room. I had begun to look forward to this period of my daily life. When meditating, I lost all sense of time and never knew how long I'd been at it, but I always felt good afterwards.

I decided to visit my mother and made my way to my grandparents' house. The three of them were stretched out in deck chairs soaking up the special tranquillity from the atmosphere of our plane. It was a picture seeing them together like this. I was about to leave, thinking it best not to disturb them, when Mum stirred and sleepily called to me.

I returned and spoke in a slight whisper: 'Sorry to disturb you, but I thought you would like to go to one of the churches we spoke of.' 'What day is it, Jim, is it Sunday?' 'No, Mum. But you can go to church here any time you wish, not just on Sunday.' 'Well, in that case, I would like to,' she replied. Ray and Charlie were still asleep, but I wanted to ask them if they would like to join us. I didn't have to disturb them because Charlie rose from his chair and came over to me. 'It's alright, Jim,' he said, 'we'll not disturb Ray. You take your mother and have a good day.'

I asked which way Mother would like to travel. She insisted that as God had given her two feet she was going to use them. This meant we had a five-mile walk ahead of us to the nearest church. Well, we started our journey, which obviously took some time; not that there was any rush. Mum also stopped every few yards to admire the view and talk to the passers-by. We eventually got to the church, and it was magnificent. A lot of thought had gone into its building. We entered through two large ornate doors. A gentleman came over to us and said, 'The service has already started. If you would like to go in, please sit at the back.'

I thanked him, and we found two seats quite close to the back. We made ourselves comfortable and focused on the sermon: 'He was always learning, loving, watching. Always out of Himself—doubling Himself up, as it were, to penetrate those realities much lower than Himself. He was never finished. What He learnt today had to be re-learnt. This was accomplished with the attitude that what He learnt was not his own mind's fancies and theories, but the qualities and habits of reality. His life thus expanded into other lives.

'What He discovered was not clear, but vivid; not simple, but rich; not readily or irresistibly transferred to other minds, but acquired only through slow purification and humble, loving observation and docility like His own. Our Lord uncovered such realities slowly, laboriously, intermittently, partially. We get to know them, not inevitably nor altogether apart from our dispositions—but only if we are sufficiently humble to welcome them and sufficiently generous to pay the price repeatedly. We get to know realities in proportion to our worthiness—proportionate to our becoming less occupied, less self-centred, more outgoing, more lost in the crowd, more rich in giving our all.

'We realize that we know these realities by our knowledge proving fruitful. All this is accomplished through practical and concrete living, not through something abstract or that can be foretold. Yet, it is always achieved in a quite inexhaustible way. We should not wait vacantly for something to happen to us by the grace of God, but should seek the grace of God by living, thinking, adventuring and praying in a definite and practical way. Thus the light that resides in every man as he comes into this world gradually flares into a flame that guides his life. It is not a vague aura of loving kindness but is the focus of all his energies, capacities, thoughts, imagination and desires.

'How shall we tend the flame? We first have to cultivate a sensitivity to value which enables us to assess by Christ's absolute standards the undertones of our daily living. We must discern unerringly that which counts most in God's eyes and that which counts most in our own. This sensitivity to value requires a delicate awareness of our motives and attitudes so that we can recognize our thought habits for exactly what they are. Why, for instance, do we hold the views we hold—for truth's sake or for comfort's sake? The Light will tell us. It will help us discern the difference between spiritual pride and goodwill, between self-righteousness and humility, between a just decision and a self-interested one, between sins to which we are inclined and sins to which we have no mind.

'One of the first signs of the light in our minds is the capacity to distinguish between the currency of a mean life and the coinage of generous living. From here, we take the first step to return to Him. This step is the first love and the first born of every creature who is himself the Light of the world. Return home to within; sweep clean your houses. You will see what the kingdom of God is like. Here you will discover that your teacher is not removed to a corner but is present always. When you are on your bed or about your labour, He is there—convincing, instructing, leading, correcting, judging and giving peace to all who love and follow Him. Not only must we return home to within, but also reach outwards to the new world about us. Here we end the lesson and may God bless the words that have been spoken. Well, my brothers and sisters, let us now stand for the next hymn, *Nearer My God to Thee.*'

My mother and I joined in with the hymn. The minister ended with a prayer and thanked the congregation for attending. We left uplifted and with a much richer knowledge.

'Thanks, Jim, for taking me,' said Mum. 'I enjoyed the service and also said a prayer for your father.' 'That's alright, Mum. As a matter of fact, I said a prayer for Dad as well.' As we made our way home, Mum was full of smiles. I was pleased to see her so happy; you would not have thought by looking at her that she had been here for such a short time. She looked extremely well. We entered my grandparents' garden and immediately were met by Charlie.

'Ah, there you are Jim,' he said. 'I have a message from your teacher. I think he said his name was Chan. Anyway, you are to go straight home.'

10

I knew it must be urgent for Chan to come looking for me. I quickly made my farewells and left Mum in Ray's capable hands. I soon stepped through the door to my house. Chan stood by the window; Harry and Jack were also awaiting my arrival. I asked what was going on.

'It is time to start your work. There have been many well-planned intrusions from the second plane into the third. We intend to purge some of these lower astrals from the earth plane, and we need as many groups as possible to stem the tide. It is gathering speed and, if we do not stop it now, there will be all-out war on the lower astral plane which will over-flow into the earth plane. As a matter of fact, it is already happening. There is general unrest on the earth, especially in Germany. Evil is entwining itself in the hearts of many who are in power. You may be wondering why we have not done anything before. We have had groups working, but keep in mind that evil is very clever and has been diverting us from its real goal. Now it has shown himself by gaining a stranglehold, and we must prise it away from the true goal. Now, gentlemen, are there any questions?'

Harry and Jack looked at me and shook their heads. 'And I don't have any,' I answered. 'This will be a long battle, gentlemen, and I wish you well,' continued Chan. His words filled our hearts with strength. I don't know why his words should have this effect, but they did.

'Now, if you are ready, we will begin.' Chan beckoned us to stand near him. He lifted his hand and made a gesture in the air. A light appeared from his palm. This was followed by a sense of movement which only lasted a few moments. When it stopped, we were in a mist which reminded me of my first trip here. The ground was very uneven; patches of brown grass sprang from the parched earth. Thank God I could leave all this behind me. There was no comparison between this place and where I lived.

There are many lost souls who wander this plane not knowing that anything lies beyond. They wander in packs, the weakest led by evil ones. The evil ones are clever because they keep the weakest away from our rescue teams by holding them by their lower natures. Slowly they get used to the mist and think it's natural. Many will stay in these conditions. Some will sink lower; others will be helped out. The desire to climb out of this hell must come from themselves. I was shaken from my thoughts by Chan's command: 'This way, gentlemen.'

'Where are we going?' enquired Jack. 'We are to meet other groups in order to work out a plan of action,' said Chan. 'We will need a plan if we are to win this battle. Now please, follow me.' Chan led us to a clearing where other groups were assembling. There must have been about two hundred people. As we waited, my mind went back to my first encounter with the lower astrals. That was some fight, but this time it seemed to be on an even larger scale. How correct my thoughts were. Chan stood to my right, with Harry and Jack to my left. I turned and asked Harry how he was feeling. 'Nervous,' he replied. 'So am I,' piped up Jack. Before I could agree with my friends Chan tapped me on the shoulder, saying 'They are ready to start.'

All eyes focussed on a shimmering light that appeared on top of a nearby large boulder. It was soon apparent that someone was materializing from it. When the figure was fully formed, I recognized the old monk from several years back. His appearance brought back the memory of his parting words from that first encounter: 'One day we will work together again.' That was a long time ago, but his words had come true. I listened intently to what he was saying now. First came words of encouragement, then an explanation of the work ahead.

'You will be placed into groups of about twenty,' he said. At the head of each group will be a soul who is well versed in this work. You will go to them for any minor decision. The leader of each group will be in constant touch with the command post where all information will be sorted. The most urgent will come to me so that I can act accordingly. Each of you will be given a coloured armband to be worn at all times. The colour will designate your group. Once you have established contact with your group, keep in constant touch with each other. Do not, on any account, wander off on your own. Always stay in pairs. If one succumbs, the other will be able to ask for help.

'Your work, my friends, is very important. We must not fail. Your groups will be delegated to specific countries. The leaders of each group will be told the name of the country and its location.

'If you look to the right of where I am standing, you will see seven flag poles. When you are given your armband, make your way to the pole flying your colour. Once there, you will be placed into smaller groups.

'Remember you have the Lord's presence with you. Did He not say, "Lo, I am with you always"? Keep this in mind as you go about your work. May God bless you and give you strength for the work ahead.'

Brother David then made the sign of the cross and spoke some words in Latin. He raised his hands high above his head, and a light appeared from them. The light intensified and spread over all of us. I sensed the immense power of Brother David as the light infused us with the love of the Christ spirit. Within minutes the light had gone, along with Brother David, but I still felt his love burning into my very soul. There it stayed and kept me going over many long years.

I turned to Chan in time to see him take three yellow armbands out of his pocket. He handed these to us to put on. We then made our way to the appropriate flag pole. An organizer stood at each flag pole to place us in our respective groups. The organizer called to the guides to come forward. Chan went forward with the others. They were in conversation for some time. Chan came back to us, and I asked what was up.

'Be patient, Jim,' he replied. 'I have been told that Germany is heading for war, and that evil has entwined itself deeply everywhere. It is so strong that we have very little hope of averting a war. Other groups have tried to get close to those in power, but the lower elements have a vast legion guarding them. Our job is not to tackle them, but to help where we can. It will be a long job, and we must be steadfast.' Chan paused for a moment then said, 'I think they are ready to address us.'

'May I please have your attention, gentlemen. Thank you. I have spoken to those who will be leading you in the fight. They will designate the location of your work. At all times you must obey their commands. Remember help will always be at hand, but use your common sense. If you come up against a situation that you cannot handle on your own, call for help. Well, good luck.'

Chan was our group's section leader, and as the leader he addressed the group before we commenced. 'You will be placed into smaller units. At the head of each unit will be a soul well versed in this work. Your names will be read out by the head of each unit. Please go to them when your name is called.'

We were soon placed in our units. Chan was not only the head of our unit but also commanded the whole group. His work would be twofold.

I thought that one war should have been enough for Germany, but it seemed they were starting all over again. Well, it was time for our work to begin. We were told to make a circle and to link hands. It was a large circle since there were forty of us in our group. The intensity of willpower was immense. I felt myself move very quickly. Then the movement stopped almost as quickly as it had begun. When everyone had recovered, we were called by our unit leaders. There were ten groups in all, and each group soon left. Only four of us remained.

'Where are we?' I asked. 'We are in the astral level of Germany,' Chan replied. 'Each of the unit leaders has been given his designated area. We are going to a place where souls are crying out for God's help.'

Harry and Jack were remarkably quiet considering what was happening. I looked towards them. They seemed alright, but I think they were a bit apprehensive about the work ahead. I knew I was.

'Right, my friends, it is time to start,' said Chan. 'Before we go, I wish to explain where we are going. You may sense some unusual conditions, ones which you may not have come across before. You may have to use your power of concentration to protect yourselves from them, but you will quickly get used to them. Until you become familiar with these new surroundings, I want you to link hands with me.'

Chan held out his hands. The three of us took hold, and we were immediately on our way. We reappeared in a place that resembled the back streets of my old earth home. I quickly sensed the conditions Chan had spoken about. It's hard to say exactly how I felt. An overwhelming sense of fear crept over me making me feel quite ill. 'Chan,' I said, 'I feel the conditions you spoke about.' 'So do I,' said Jack. 'Me too,' echoed Harry. 'That is to be expected,' said Chan. 'Do as you were taught, and cleanse your aura. Wait, I will help.' I sensed Chan's immense willpower as he concentrated on us. Within moments the conditions had no effect on us.

'That's better,' said Harry. 'I'm ready to begin now.' 'Yes,' said Jack, 'so am I.' If we had known what we were letting ourselves in for, we would not have been so eager.

'This way,' said Chan. We followed him along cobbled streets until we stopped outside a Victorian-style, three storey house. The house had a foreboding feeling about it. Chan beckoned us to follow inside so we entered the house. Chan immediately climbed the stairs. We followed him into a room that was at the top of the house. The door to the room was hidden from sight by a bookcase, but as we were not part of the earth's physical laws, we were able to walk straight through it. The room was sparsely furnished. There were several makeshift beds, one or two with people asleep in them, and a group of five people sitting around a small table. I asked Chan who they were.

'These souls,' he said, 'dared to speak out against the regime. Now they are paying the price. They are being hunted and, most certainly, will be caught and put to death. That is why we are here.'

'How cruel,' said Harry. 'It makes me feel sick,' replied Jack. 'How do you know they will be caught?' I asked. 'It is in the order of things,' Chan replied. 'We will have to wait here until the time is right.'

I took a closer look around the room. In one of the corners two children played on the floor. They were very thin and pale, but looked contented enough. I'm sure they had no idea what was about to happen to them. Thank God they didn't.

'It is beginning,' said Chan. I stepped forward to where Chan and my two friends stood. The air chilled around us, and the little light we had began to fade. My heart started to race, and I felt agitated. Suddenly, the door burst open and a young man ran in shouting at the top of his voice, 'The Nazis are here. God help us.'

The mother of the two children rushed over to them and cradled them in her arms as she cried uncontrollably. The others huddled in the centre of the room. Most were on their knees in prayer. I saw the intensity of their prayers as they asked for God's help. I also sensed their fear.

I was startled by the loud crashing of a downstairs door and the sound of many heavy feet on the staircase. As the noise came closer, the wailing of the group grew stronger until it was unbearable. I wanted to shut it out, but couldn't. I knew I had to stand my ground and wait. The coldness intensified and black vapour appeared in the ether around us. The door to the room suddenly crashed open, and four men in black uniforms carrying guns entered. Behind them came figures of a malign nature. These creatures were dead to the earth world but dominated their earthly counterparts. As soon as they caught sight of us, they rushed forwards with outstretched hands which looked more like talons. Before I knew it, three of these creatures were on top of me, hitting, biting and clawing away at my flesh. I managed to push them off, but the pain they inflicted made me angry. I could not fight with my fists, but by God I could fight with my mind. I concentrated all my will-power on creating a shield of light around myself. The next moment I heard one of the creatures scream out in pain as he reeled back from the band of light. The fight came to a sudden end; we had won. The evil creatures disappeared from our sight.

There was a heavy mist in the room. I heard the sound of gunfire. We had to wait for the mist to clear before we could see what had happened. Slowly my sight adjusted. There was no movement whatsoever. The men in uniforms had gone, leaving the bodies of the dead and dying; even the two children lay on the floor. 'No,' I shouted, 'how can this be?' 'Control yourself,' Chan barked. 'You will gain strength as we go on. Our work is not yet over. We have to wait.'

I looked over to Harry and Jack. By the look on their faces, they felt pretty much the same as I did. How could any human being do this to such defenceless people? When evil strikes, it strikes with a vengeance such as I had just witnessed. As I watched the bodies of these poor souls, a mist formed over the top of them. The astral bodies began to form. It was our job to get them away from this place as quickly as possible. The first to break away from their bodies were the two children, who looked dazed. I immediately went to them and gathered them into my arms. I took them to where Chan was standing.

'Wait a moment, Jim,' said Chan. 'I am sending for some help.' Chan became silent and went into a state of deep thought, but he was soon back with us. 'Well, that's done,' he said. 'They should be here soon.'

The children started to get restless. 'I want my mummy,' said one. The other one started to cry. I had never had anything to do with children before, and I didn't know what to do. I cradled them tightly to my chest and sang to them. My singing must have fascinated them because they stopped crying. Two shapes materialized next to Chan. This startled the two youngsters, and they began to cry again.

The two materialized forms were nurses. They walked over to me. 'Here, let us take the bonny lasses for ye,' said one in a very broad Scottish accent. Within moments the children were pacified. I admired the nurses' way with children.

Harry shouted from across the room to me: 'We need some help over here.' Harry and Jack were arguing with some of the new astrals. I went across to them and asked what was the matter. 'They don't believe they're dead,' said Harry. 'Oh, don't they?' I said. 'Well I can assure you, you are dead. Well, dead to the earth plane anyway. So please don't argue, not for now anyway. Just come with us, and we will lead you away from here to somewhere better.'

The look on their faces was one of amazement as we led them to Chan. The last thing they expected was to be presented to a Chinaman. After a few words from Chan, they stood by rather passively. We managed to gather all the souls quickly, except one. The mother of the two children still held on to her earth body. I heard Chan talking to one of the nurses, 'I think she is in a state of shock.'

The nurse agreed, and both the nurses went over to where she lay. They bent over the body, one at the head and the other at the feet. I could not quite make out what they were doing, but they were there for some time. They then moved away from the body and waited. Five minutes passed, and a mist appeared over the body. When the astral body had formed, the two nurses took charge and stood her on her feet. She was in a terrible state of shock, shaking violently. I heard her calling through her tears: 'My babies, where are my babies?' She kept repeating the same words; nothing else seemed to matter, not even the fact that she was dead. She was led over to Chan and the others. 'Right,' said Chan. 'We have them all.'

He ordered us to stand around the group. When we were all in position, Chan raised his hand. A light emanated from the palm of his hand and encircled us. When the light lifted, we were in a hospital. We were immediately met by several nurses who took charge of the souls we had brought. The mother and two children were reunited; not even death could separate them for long. I thanked God they were safe here from the evil on the earth plane. When everything had been sorted out, Chan took us to one side and said how pleased he was with us.

11

Our work continued in the astral level of Germany for some years. Germany was well into war by then. Many souls came to this side of life long before their time. We had many encounters with the lower astrals; each time I became stronger. We went home for periods of rest, but not for long. The war would not stop for us to rest.

Chan called a meeting of the whole group. 'There are certain places in Germany where sheer barbarism is occurring. To get near, the whole group must work together. Evil is using these places to manifest fear and feeds on this fear for the strength to manifest its evil ways on earth. I have one more thing to say before we go. Be strong in the work to come. It will be nothing like the encounters you have experienced before.'

I later realized how correct Chan's words were. Chan led us in prayer. He then took the group to a most dreary location—a place full of evil intent. 'This, my friends, will be the battleground,' continued Chan. 'If you look ahead, you will see the place we are to attack.'

A light mist covered everything, making it difficult to see. When my eyes pierced the mist, I saw a very large black wall some twenty to thirty feet away from where we stood. 'Come,' said Chan, 'we will walk around it.' We covered eight to ten miles and discovered that the wall formed a square with no means of entry. I was glad we stood some distance away because I could sense the tremendous force of evil and fear behind the wall.

'How on earth are we to get in there?' I asked. 'Wait, and I will show you,' Chan answered. He called the group to order. 'Now, gentlemen. Would you please make one straight line.' This was difficult because of the mist and because there were so many of us, but we managed. Chan then took the first three in line and then the next three. He placed them at the head of the line into the shape of an arrowhead. Chan was to be the point.

'We shall gain entry by this formation,' he said. 'We are the arrow, and the Light shall be the bow. I want all of you to use your willpower to create light around yourselves.' Each of us did as Chan asked, with a most unusual effect. The power generated by the group was tremendous. It nearly lifted us off the ground. 'Right,' said Chan, 'if you are ready, we will begin.'

As we approached the wall I sensed a heaviness, but the arrow pierced through. It was heavy going, similar to swimming against the tide. We penetrated the wall, and left a hole that could easily be walked through. The sight inside was enough to turn the stomachs of the hardest of men. There were hundreds of souls walking aimlessly around. Zombies is the only way to describe these souls who were dead to the earth world but could not escape from this madhouse. Even after death they were held here by the evil elements. New souls joined them every minute. It was a camp of death.

Chan barked out his orders, which brought me back to the job at hand. 'Be on guard,' he said. 'There are enemies about. Once they realize we have broken through, there will certainly be a war.' Chan spoke none too soon. From out of nowhere several lower astrals attacked us. They were the guards, not the main force, and were no match for us. We quickly drove them back.

'Right,' said Chan, 'start directing these souls through the hole in the wall.' What started as a trickle soon became a flood. Many of them shouted out, 'Look! the light, the light. We are saved.' 'Not yet,' I thought. 'How on earth were we going to help all these people?' There were hundreds of them rushing towards us. They still held the fear that they had been made to suffer. It intensified by the minute and almost devoured me in the onslaught. I asked for God's help.

'No time for those thoughts,' said Chan, 'get on with the work.' I don't know how many passed through the wall, but many hundreds still gathered around us. I turned to Chan and said, 'We need help.' 'I have it under control,' he replied. 'Many of our friends are outside directing operations.' I felt better knowing we had more friends about. The battle was not yet over with the lower astrals. They re-grouped, but this time they had more evil beings with them. They were the same kind we had fought in the drinking den many years earlier. I quickly turned to Chan and said, 'I don't think we will be able to beat them back this time.'

'You are right,' he said. 'There are too many for us to tackle. We need help.' Chan stopped, closed his eyes and concentrated. A minute or two passed before he opened his eyes. 'Help is on the way,' he said. 'Let's hope it arrives soon,' I replied. There must have been a note of desperation in my voice because suddenly Chan's willpower joined mine and recharged me.

The lower astrals came towards us at a steady pace. They

stopped to size up the situation. As soon as they realized there were only a few of us, they rushed at us. They were pushed forward by evil creatures who never enter the fight. They were there to suck up the negative emotions of the battle. Their auras were black with flashes of crimson running through. As they sucked up the emotions their auras changed to pure black. Within minutes the lower astrals were on top of us. They attacked us with such a ferocity that we were pushed back towards the wall. On seeing this battle, the souls we had come to help fled in all directions. It was a double shock for the poor souls to see these evil creatures come from nowhere.

One of our group fell. Within moments the lower astrals were on top of him. I fought my way over to him and jumped into the brawl. They were getting the better of us when suddenly they started to pull back. 'What's making them give up?' I asked the chap I was helping. 'Look over there,' he sighed and pointed towards the wall.

Whole portions of the wall disintegrated, revealing our army and friends. On seeing what was happening, they entered the fight. The battle raged for a long time. The evil astrals had a new-found ferocity. Neither side gave or gained ground. Suddenly the darkness was pierced by a wave of white fire. It was followed by another, and another, shedding a great light over the whole camp. It was so bright it hurt my eyes, and I quickly closed them. From the sound of their screams the light must have had a tremendous effect on the lower astrals. I gently opened my eyes in time to see what was happening. In every direction I looked the lower astrals were trying to hide from the light. The most evil of the creatures deserted the lower astrals to let them fend for themselves. There was nowhere for them to run. They could only hide amongst the newly slain, but they were easy to distinguish and could be sorted out later.

I wanted to find Chan so I scanned the battlefield. He was talking to a group of friends. I made my way to him. In the midst of the fighting he had lost his hat, and his clothes were torn. When he had finished talking I asked about the great lights we had just seen. 'They, my young friend,' he said, 'were the Lords of Light I have spoken of. Now you have seen their work for yourself. They came to battle with the powers of evil and have won. Right, I have a little job for you while I direct operations here. I want you to take a search party and go into the camp. You are to seek out the souls who may be hiding from us out of fear.'

A group of six friends approached us. 'Good, you are here,' said Chan. He introduced us and told us to leave no stone unturned in our search.

We made our way around the encampment and directed those who were lost and dazed to safety. As we went deeper into the encampment, we felt the fear increase. We knew by this that there were more souls in hiding. We came across several huts and entered one of them. It was a type of dormitory, with bunk beds along both sides. There must have been over a hundred beds. The fear that emanated from this room was overpowering, but we had learnt to cope with this. We started our search, splitting up to cover more of the area.

One of us soon indicated he had found some of the souls we were looking for. We managed to pacify them and led them to safety. Our search went on for many hours. Finally, I came to a dormitory that would change the course of events for me. In my search I came across the soul of a young boy. He was about ten or eleven years old. He looked a pitiful sight huddled in one of the darkest corners so that no one could see his naked body. His eyes had sunk deep into their sockets. There was very little flesh on his frail skeleton. His body was held together by the arteries and veins that had once given life to a healthy child.

Something snapped inside me, and I fell on my knees. I was overcome by the immense emotion of the battle, and I deeply regretted belonging to the human race. It was this pitiful child that brought reality home to me. My head hung down in shame. Bitterness and hatred welled up inside me. I had not felt this way for many years. I wanted to get hold of just one of the human beings who had inflicted this on one so young. I did not feel one bit spiritual. By God, it showed as I hammered the floor with my fists. I suddenly felt a cold hand on my shoulder. I looked up into the eyes of the child, who had come over to where I knelt. I looked deep into the pitiful eyes. They looked like two large pools of water. I was so overcome by this child that I grabbed hold of him and pulled him to my chest. Love poured from me into him, and he responded in the only way he knew. He placed his arms around my neck and held on to me for all he was worth.

'Don't worry,' I said. 'You're safe now. No one will ever hurt you again.' I picked him up and made my way to Chan. Thank God I didn't meet any lower astrals on the way—not for my sake, but theirs.

Chan took one look at us and said, 'I understand, Jim. It's time you left here. There is another job to be done, but I will accompany you. There are other children here who must be taken to the children's sphere. Wait here for me to round them up.'

Chan was gone for some time. The child was asleep in my arms. Nothing was going to prise him away from me, not for now anyway. I looked in the direction Chan had gone and caught sight of him leading a bunch of children towards me. They too were as naked as the day they were born. Chan had hold of the hands of two of the children. When they came close enough, I saw the horror that had been inflicted on these defenceless children.

I realized months later that this period of my life was a testing time. Even though I was in a state of shock, I learnt much. In fact, rescuing the children evoked my desire to relay all of this to you. Chan approached me, saying, 'Come, Jim. We will go now.'

There were twenty-two children in all. Many more followed. The children stood motionless as Chan waved his hand. A light emanated from his palm and encircled us. When the light had gone, we stood inside a magnificent building. 'Where are we?' I asked. 'In the children's sphere,' he answered.

I heard the sound of running feet on the marble floor. A large group of nurses and nuns hurried towards us. As they approached they didn't speak, but took hold of the children and pulled them to their bosoms. I noticed one or two of the nurses had tears rolling down their cheeks as they fussed over the children. One young nurse came up to me and asked for the child I had in my arms. I was hesitant to hand him over, and he was equally hesitant to let go. I held on to him as long as I could, but my heart told me he was safe here. I battled with myself, but I did not have to make the decision. It was made for me. Chan tapped me on the shoulder: 'Let her take him. He will be in good hands, and you will be able to visit him whenever you like.'

I handed him over to the nurse, whose aura oozed with love for my young friend. Her angelic face made the boy and myself feel at ease. I kissed him on the forehead and said I would see him soon. As the nurse walked away, he waved to me. 'What's your name young fellow?' I asked. 'John,' he shouted back.

'I'll be seeing you soon, John,' I reminded him. 'Be good and do as they ask.' He smiled, and they walked out of sight. I felt some relief knowing that the children were now being well looked after.

I turned to Chan and asked if he could tell me more about where we were. 'We call this the children's sphere,' he said. 'That is exactly what it is. Children are brought here to be educated in the ways of the higher life. Many have come here through war, such as the ones we brought. Others are here because they were not loved on earth and can now experience maternal love. There are many other reasons I could give. The Blue Sisterhood is a special women's organization that deals with these children. The women, when on earth, either never married or were married but childless for one reason or another. They would have made wonderful mothers, but as the opportunity passed them by, their desires followed them into this world. Here they can fully utilize their motherly instincts. There are many institutions like this one in this sphere because many thousands of children come here daily—which gives you some idea of the immensity of this sphere.'

'What about their parents?' I asked. 'I was just coming to that,' he said. 'When a child dies before his parents, he is brought here for re-education. In that education, the child is allowed to go with a guardian to the earth plane to keep watch over his parents' progress. When the time is right, the family will be reunited. The ones who die during war will, with their parents, enter a transitional period. They will then be reunited in the most suitable sphere for their family's progression.'

'I think I understand,' I said. 'Do you think the nuns or nurses would mind if I looked around?' I asked. 'Of course not,' Chan replied, 'let me accompany you.'

We walked along a large, panelled corridor. Chan stopped occasionally to point out interesting parts of the cornice. Everything was remarkably well thought out; every part of the decor blended. We approached a pair of ornate panelled doors. On opening the doors, I was dumbfounded at the beauty that surrounded us. Wonderful gardens seemed to spring from the deep green grass. I have said 'spring' because I felt it was impossible that man could have created such a cascade of colour. The gardens spread for miles in every direction. Trees covered with roses and other flowering creepers enclosed the gardens.

'Come,' said Chan, 'let us walk.' We walked along a broad, grass road. I stopped several times to take in the beauty of the flowers. Groups of young children played happily in the sprawling gardens. Nuns were teaching groups of the older children. I was pleased to see that the children's education was not being neglected. Chan agreed they were getting a good education.

'You're reading my thoughts again,' I commented. We both smiled. We continued along the road until we came to a clearing. In the centre of the clearing was a sculpture group of

Jesus with outstretched arms above the heads of three children. I bent down and read the plaque beneath the statue: 'Suffer little children to come unto me.' How appropriate those words were. This great soul showed His love for His children, young and old, by always being open to receive them. The sculpture reminded me to ask Chan if there would be a second coming on earth.

'He is already there,' Chan replied, 'but has not been recognized.' 'What? You mean He has been reborn?' I asked. 'Yes, in an indirect way,' he replied. 'Chan, you're talking in riddles.' 'I suppose I am,' he said, 'but my words are true. Now let me explain. Christ is not on the cross now. His death is history. He has risen and ascended on high. The throne of grace is not the crucifix or the confessional, it is where Christ sits—at the right hand of God. Those who believe in heart and mind may ascend and dwell continually with Him. But this is not the whole story. Many do not realize the Lord is within every child who is starving or being mistreated. Look into the eyes of one of these children. There you will see the Lord. Yes, He has been reborn, but He has not been recognized.'

We talked for some time on this subject, then I asked Chan about what would happen to John. 'He will be looked after,' he said. 'First, they will bathe and clothe him. Then he will rest. They do not have the worry of weaning him off food. His astral mind has already accepted his condition. In place of food for the stomach, he will be fed the food of love. In a short time he will have adjusted to his new home—just as the children we saw playing. When you visit him, you will be surprised to see the change in him.'

We spent hours taking in the beauty of this sphere. We stopped occasionally to chat with some of the children. Chan finally indicated it was time for us to leave.

12

'I think it would be nice to have a bathe,' said Chan. 'I was just going to say the same thing,' I replied. 'Before you say anything,' Chan remarked, 'I have not been reading your mind.'

We laughed; our way of thinking was becoming unusually similar. I took a final look at the scenery before we left. On reappearing by the pool, Chan immediately undressed and entered the water. I soon followed. It was good to recharge my batteries; I felt better. 'I do as well,' said Chan. It's quite a strange feeling having someone read your innermost thoughts. Time slipped by. Chan was content to float on the water and relax.

'I have a question, and I thought perhaps...' Before I could finish what I was saying, Chan replied, 'Well, what is your question?' 'I was thinking about the leaders of Germany. What will happen to them when they come to this side of life?' My question must have flummoxed Chan. He stood up and placed his hand on his chin and held this pensive pose for several minutes.

'A good question,' he finally said. Chan paused again before speaking. 'They will gravitate to their own level of spiritual awareness. Do keep in mind that the evil these beings have inflicted on their brothers and sisters will eventually come back to them. That is the law of "karma". In God's wisdom they will be given a chance to make amends for the cruelty they have inflicted. It will take a long time, Jim, for them to work out their karma.'

'But, surely, these souls are beyond help,' I said. 'They certainly are not,' replied Chan sharply. 'I'm sorry,' I said. 'I did not mean to offend you.' 'No apologies are necessary,' he replied. 'You must understand that they too are God's children. Like any naughty child, they must be taught a lesson. This will be accomplished by their incarnating into certain situations which will give them the appropriate experience. They will suffer and experience what they inflicted on others.'

'It's all very complicated,' I said. 'I've heard about reincarnation before, but I have never understood it.' Chan replied, 'I did not say they would reincarnate. I said they would incarnate, and, as you are aware, there are many states of being. The best thing to do is to go to a lecture on the subject. Wait a moment, I will find out when and where the next lecture is to be given.' Chan closed his eyes and went into a state of concentration. A few minutes passed before he opened his eyes and said: 'A lecture is beginning shortly. If we hurry, we will be in time.'

We dressed, and Chan directed us by thought to the outside of a large marble building. 'Where are we?' I asked. Chan replied, 'We are standing outside one of the halls of learning. This particular hall is well known for its fine lectures. Many people come each day to study the ways of the greater life. That is enough talking, or we will be late.'

We climbed several steps to two large golden doors with panels of embossed eagles with outstretched talons. I glanced around the magnificent hall, but we did not have time to take in the whole environment. Chan led me through one of the many doors that surrounded the lecture theatre. The seats were set out in a circle. It reminded me of a Roman amphitheatre. We were lucky to find two empty seats. I had no chance to say anything to Chan because the speaker already stood in the centre of the auditorium. He was handsomely dressed in the style of a Greek philosopher. Even from where we sat, I sensed an air of respect about him. He introduced himself and went straight into the lecture.

'The question "Do we reincarnate?" is understood and answered in the affirmative by the seekers of spiritual truth. Others will argue vehemently against this. It has become a question that divides many minds and creates voids between parties. This adds up to a good discussion, which should not be considered a bad thing. Unfortunately, it is reaching a stalemate. We, on the spirit plane, now feel it would be wise to introduce a further factor into the discussion. it is already known but has not been drawn into the debates.

'There are many layers of endeavour or planes of expression that are known and accepted by spiritual seekers—lower astral, astral, and the first to the fourth, and the true planes of spirit. The means by which entities (man) are able to pass from plane to plane is not often understood. The existence of similar planes of expression within the structure of material or manifested states of existence (earthlike) such as rocks, lichens, plants, insects, birds and animals is totally overlooked. Another point left out of the discussion is the soul's descent through various layers before its initial incarnation as man or woman in the manifested plane of expression.

'You now understand that the physical expressions of matter are not life's realities. You must also grasp that it is impossible for a manifestation on one plane to pass in its entirety into the next plane for its return circuit. The bulk usually stays behind. This seems to be the difficulty for most people's understanding of the full meaning behind reincarnation.

'It has deliberately been made difficult for matter to pass from one plane to another, and it can only be done by the method known as "spiritualization". This means that matter must reach a stage of perfection as understood by that plane before it can transmute to the next. This can only be accomplished with the aid of matter that has knowledge of how to manage the transition. This knowledge has been acquired by matter mastering the technique at an early stage. This assisting agent is called a layer-of-soul or higher state of expression. This principle is legion throughout all states of expression. *All life forms* have a higher inner-self.

'Soul consists of a centre of intensity surrounded by layers of varying degrees of attainment. That is to say by layers of spiritualized matter which have reached a certain state of evolution and are unable to proceed further on their own abilities. In order to make further progress, the soul must serve its lower outer layers. These layers are picked up by the descending soul and outbirthed to the next lower plane of expression which the soul needs for its own fulfilment. In the orders below man, soul work is generally carried out on a group principle.

'The evolving essence of a particular species is held collectively by an overlord agent which is the central principle of that species from which all body matter of the species comes for each separate incarnation of that species such as the ant, bee, plant, etc. The group soul of each branch of each species (and there are many) is, or forms part of, a layer of the overall group soul or oversoul which may not have its being in or around the planet earth. It may be part of the soul of some other planet within our solar system. Our planet, or mother nature, is also a group soul. It is made up of and holds all unevolved matter which is used to make the outer body of all living things on the earth including man and the rocks. Even the rocks must evolve.

'It may take the lifetime of this solar system before its first change from rock. Until each order evolves and is able to pass into its spiritual plane, it is brought back again and again by the group soul until it has sufficiently raised its vibrational rate to a usable level for the higher group soul to form a lower part of the next order of being. The group soul does not reincarnate. It only holds and aids the evolution of the matter of its manifestating state, for example a bird or bee. It is interesting to note that the bees not only help the flowers by pollination, but they also spiritualize the nectar by turning it into honey. All true evolution takes place within the spirit plane of the species, not on the manifested plane, and is always only a reflection of its associate soul. This process occurs on all planes of expression lower than man.

'Each spiritual plane is now known by its manifesting plane. The physical plane of man is an exception to this rule. He enters as an individual on this plane of expression. Having said that, the soul still belongs to a group soul and the order of that soul's progress. The progress of any relevant matter, as explained previously, applies to man also. The only difference is that he personalizes because he has conscious awareness that he exists.

'Most orders below man have no knowledge of self, although there is a varying degree of knowledge, or a twilight awareness, in some of the higher orders of species. There is a constant exchange of evolved essence of the lower orders throughout the evolving order of all expressions. It percolates slowly to higher states of expression. It is aided by group souls who percolate in their turn from group soul to group soul. The essence thus evolves until it is suitable for use by man, man to angel, angel to God.

'It is not possible in any state of being for evolved energy to go backwards. Once it has reached a certain level of vibration, or perfection as some like to say, it transmutes to a higher order of being. The essence of matter progresses only onward and upward, until it is spiritualized by man. It then progresses to the true plane of spirit away from the earth plane. By using everything around him, man aids spiritualization of all the lower orders. As stated earlier, the progress of man's person-alized, spiritualized matter is similar to that of the lower or unspiritualized states. I am using this expression to help you differentiate between various states of being, their order and their changing from one state to another. It is essential to have this understanding clearly in your mind. You will then be able to picture, as clearly as possible, the events pertaining to the evolutionary flow of matter up to and into the state of man and beyond.

'In addition to being able to differentiate states of being, it is essential to recognize the similarity of all fields of progress. The principle, which not only man but all must follow, requires a flow from sphere to sphere, or plane to plane. Therefore all reincarnation is within each plane, and not from plane to plane as held by those who argue for its existence, and disputed by those who do not believe. It is difficult to explain the next process without leaving out vital parts, or becoming so obscure as to fail to convey the purpose of this lecture. In an attempt to be as lucid as possible, I will start at the end and finish at the end.

'In order that the lowest order may evolve, it must and can only be served by a higher order. The soul was created for this purpose. The soul has a higher state of knowledge than the matter that forms its outer shell. It is formed by soul matter held on progressive planes and vibrates at the different rates through which it must pass. This should not be considered contradictory to the earlier statement on reincarnation. At this level, matter has changed essence and is essentially different.

'The spiritualized matter forms the layer of the soul. On the eventual reaching of its group soul-centre or Godhead, it is baptized and transmuted into self on the return circuit. This self forms around a centre of knowledge of the group soul's purpose. The group centre is part of a layer of an even larger group soul which will have at its centre a similar centre or "I" consciousness, *ad infinitum*. The central "I" consciousness is the Godhead of that group soul.

'In principle, all souls are made this way. This is how a seed forms into a flower. The sun baptizes the flower, and the new souls or seeds form and descend into the soil to start again. The flower arising from a seed is the highest evolutionary state on the earth of that matter. It is the seed's spirit plane and has been prepared by organisms in the earth such as slime moulds, fungi and insects for spiritualization. The plant itself is the outer layer of the soul of the flower. Above us, on the higher planes of spirit, is an organization of which we will eventually form a flowerhead to be baptized by the Light of Life.

'On the completion of the transmuted or evolved soul matter, you will stand at the Godhead where all that you have refined in your aeons of existence as an aware being will be baptized. The refined "you" will have become what is called a "Germic Self", which will have at its centre its own "I" consciousness. It is this which makes man unique on the earth plane. It gives him his conscious awareness. This, and only this, makes him aware that he *is* this. It leads him ever on to God, back to the centre of his creation. This is the seed of your flower. It must descend in order to evolve some of what you have left undone, or to complete a new purpose. Only it and the Godhead will know. You will continue on, ever on, into new states of being. The lecture is now at an end, my friends. I am open to your questions.'

The discussion went on for some time. I was impressed with the whole thing and came away from the hall more knowledgeable than when I entered. It was a little over my head, but I knew I would retain what had been said for later consideration.

We came out of the building and down the steps. I turned to Chan and said, 'Thanks for bringing me. Although I was never one for learning, it was not for want of trying. I just could not concentrate.' Chan stopped at the last step and indicated that he would like to sit on one of the benches that surrounded the building. We walked over and made ourselves comfortable.

Chan spoke: 'You must study, observe and think if your spirituality is to have any worth. Consciousness is knowledge, and knowledge comes through mental effort. The intellect and reasoning powers cannot give you life, but they can open the doors for wisdom and life to enter. Spirituality divorced from wisdom becomes fanaticism. The spirit is a seed planted in the earth body, and it grows through the earth body. It unfolds with the help of the atmosphere, turns its flower towards the all-powerful sun, and sheds its fragrance on all who come within its reach.

'The spirit of man needs both the mental and the physical for its development. But these two alone cannot bring you into the light of spiritual life. Spirituality is not just temporal living, nor is it just dreaming. It is not only for self-upliftment, nor for dwelling solely in the transcendental. All this is included, but it is something much more. It is something so great, so powerful, that the whole of life, both on the earth plane and here, is affected by it.

'Experience is necessary for the progress of the spirit. It must act, it must achieve, it must attain. It cannot expand alone. It must endeavour to help those wounded in the struggle of life, to lift others with itself and strive for their upliftment as well as its own. This is the reason you must study. Your life is an experience in itself, and your experiences will push you along the road of life.'

13

'Now, I have to get back to my work,' Chan said. 'There is some mopping up to be done in the encampment. You may come along, if you wish, or take more time to rest.'

I fell straight into his trap. I said that nothing could keep me away. Chan had a smile from ear to ear as he jumped to his feet: 'I hoped you would come back with me. I did not want you falling into a state of depression. I know it has been a shock to you, but you have coped very well with all that you witnessed in the dark regions of man's madness. If you are ready, we shall go.'

We reappeared in the encampment. Most of the inmates were gone except a few who were being led out. I noticed there were now many nurses in attendance. They too looked as if they had been in the battle. Chan led me to another part of the encampment where the lower astrals from the battle were being guarded. There must have been over three hundred of them. Most of them still suffered from the effects of the fight. Others were on their knees crying out in fear of the great light which had been inflicted on them by the Lords of Light.

Many higher astrals surrounded them to ensure none escaped before they had been talked to by one of the teachers. I turned to Chan and asked: 'Who will be addressing these souls?' Before Chan could answer, Brother David appeared in a clearing just twenty feet from where we stood. 'How is he going to talk with so much noise?' I asked. 'Wait and see,' replied Chan.

Brother David lifted his hand and made the sign of the cross. I then heard his voice inside my head. He was using telepathy to reach all of the lower astrals. I listened to his words: 'You are fast heading towards hell. If you do not repent, you will seal your fate. Think very carefully about what I am saying before it is too late. You will not be given another opportunity such as this. Those of you who want our help, make your way to my right. You will be taken away from here and given help.'

Brother David paused to allow a small stream of astrals to congregate at his right side. Other astrals tried to hold them back, but the higher astrals stepped in. The lower astrals were then led away. Brother David started to speak again. 'You have been given the opportunity to climb out of your hell, and you have not taken it. You have condemned yourselves to your own fate.'

I sensed an awesome power building up around Brother David as he concentrated his will on the remaining astrals. He spoke again, but this time the force of his will was far more intense. 'In the name of the most High and by the might of Christ, we bid you lie in the realms of night. Lie there and come no more until your astral bodies melt and fall. Then may the good Lord remember you.'

Brother David then lifted his hand, and a light began to emanate from his palm. The lower astrals became fearful as the light emanating from Brother David encircled them. They panicked and tried to break out of the cordon that was placed around them, but the light had a dramatic effect on them.

They faded from sight, never to be seen again until the good Lord decides otherwise. They were gone within a few moments. Only the soldiers of light remained in the camp. This seemed a fitting name for us. We had battled the forces of darkness and won.

I looked around for Chan but couldn't see him anywhere. I assumed he was busy. I decided to look for Harry and Jack, and turned the camp upside down in my search for them, but they were nowhere to be found. Instead, I found Chan and asked if I could be of use.

'Yes, you can,' he said. 'Very soon we will move from here, but there are still souls who are being forced over to our life before their rightful time. We are going to leave a large party of workers to help the new souls who come to this camp of death.'

'But what about the forces of darkness? Won't they try to attack us again?' I asked. 'No,' answered Chan. 'They have lost this camp and will not trouble us any more. They will build up their forces at a different location. One day there will be a great confrontation between us. Until that day, we will have the measure of them wherever we meet.'

Chan paused and then asked how I was feeling. 'Better by the minute,' I replied. 'I was wondering about Harry and Jack. I have searched the camp for them. Do you know where they are?' 'I have sent them along with some others on a mission. They should return soon,' Chan replied. 'Wait, I am receiving a message.' Chan became silent. I had seen him go into a state of concentration on many occasions. Generally, it did not last long. True to form, Chan soon nodded and said: 'There are more souls coming from the house of death.'

'Don't they realize that taking these people's lives is wrong?' I asked. 'It is difficult to say. God only knows what drives people to do these things to their fellow countrymen. Eventually, they will pay for the suffering they have inflicted on these poor souls. Right, Jim, here they come.'

I looked where Chan pointed. A large group walked our way with help from the soldiers of light. They had no clothes on their shattered bodies. Mothers still held children to their breasts hoping to save them. There was no salvation for man, woman or child from this hell that existed solely for the destruction of the human race. We could liberate these souls only after death, but their mental scars would remain with them forever.

Nurses met them as they passed through the opening in the wall. The look of relief when they saw the nurses' angelic faces was incredible. They were finally safe and would be looked after.

I heard my name being called and looked around to find Harry immediately behind me. He almost lifted me off my feet as he pulled me to his chest. He greeted me as if I were a long-lost brother. 'We have a lot to discuss,' he said. 'After the fight we lost contact with you. Were you alright?'

'I had a little trouble,' I replied and quickly changed the subject because I didn't want Harry to think I couldn't cope. 'What has become of Jack?' I asked. 'Oh, he'll be along soon. He's just finishing off,' Harry replied. 'We encountered more of the enemy than expected. They put up stiff resistance, but we soon got the better of them and sent them off on their heels.'

Harry had just finished talking when Chan walked over to

us. 'Did everything go to plan, Harry?' he asked. 'Yes, we achieved what we set out to do,' Harry replied. 'Good,' said Chan. 'When Jack returns, I have another task for the three of you.' We talked for about half an hour before Jack appeared. 'Good to see you again, Jim. Hello, Harry. We've finished the little job you gave us, Chan.'

It was an effort for Jack to get his words out. He looked tired and pale. The work had taken its toll, but I gave him full marks for keeping his composure like an officer. Chan had also noticed Jack's condition. He placed his hands on him and concentrated. Within moments, Jack's appearance changed. The deep ridges on his brow faded, and his old look returned.

'That is better,' said Chan. 'Next time do not let your batteries run down. We cannot have you going sick, can we? Now let us get back to the job at hand. Your next mission is to join a group of workers who are at present at a different location on the astral plane. You will find that a great battle has taken place. There will be many souls walking around in the mist, not realizing they are dead. Your task will be to convince them otherwise. If you are ready, we will begin.'

We soon arrived in a different place but were still on the third astral plane. The mist was much thicker, but our training enabled us to see through it. We waited until a group of twelve other soldiers appeared from the mist. At the head of the group was a very familiar figure. Harry nudged me and said, 'I've seen this bloke somewhere before.'

'Of course you have,' remarked Jack. Before Jack could give his name, the group was on top of us. The officer stepped forward and introduced himself, 'Good-day, gentlemen. My name is Captain Marsh.' He then introduced us to each of the soldiers under his command. When Chan felt all was well, he left for his work in the encampment. Captain Marsh called us to order and explained something of our work.

'I have asked for the best,' he said. 'I am sure that's what you are. There has been a great battle not far from here. Of course many have passed to our side of life. Our job is to get them away from the battlefield because the fighting still rages around them. If we don't, the lower astrals will get hold of them, and you know what will happen.' He was correct. My friends and I had experienced enough to know what would happen to these new souls.

'Right then,' continued the officer. 'We will split into five groups of three. I will leave you to decide who works with whom.' I turned to Harry and Jack and asked, 'Are we together in this?' Harry smiled and nodded. 'But, of course,' remarked Jack.

The groups were formed, and we moved off. We walked deeper into the mist towards the sounds of battle. Shadowy forms appeared, only to disappear just as quickly. We were called to a halt. The officer gave us a few words of encouragement, and the group divided to set about the work.

Harry, Jack and I went at a tangent from the rest. Our orders were to help anyone who needed it. We stayed close together knowing that the three of us would be able to cope with whatever faced us. We approached a wooded area. There was a foreboding feeling about the place—no sign of battle, just a feeling of being watched. Suddenly, a voice screamed at us from out of the mist: 'Halt, put your hands up. Sprekendy English?'

We immediately turned towards the voice. We were confronted by two British soldiers with their rifles firmly fixed on us. They seemed nervy and had obviously mistaken us for the enemy. Jack's voice boomed out: 'Put those rifles down. Don't you recognize an officer when you see one?'

This took the two soldiers by surprise. One turned in bewilderment to the other and asked: 'What do you think, George?' The other replied: 'Don't know, Fred. Can't see nothing proper through this confounded mist. You keep them covered, and I'll take a closer look. You there, keep your hands where I can see them.'

He edged his way over to us. I don't mind telling you, I was a little afraid because the soldier's gun was pointing directly at me. He looked me up and down and went across to Jack, who took hold of the barrel of the rifle and pushed it away. 'Well, private, have you had a good look?' Jack asked.

'Yes, sir,' mumbled the soldier. 'I'm sorry, sir, but you can't be too careful in this mist.' He turned towards his friend, who also kept a very watchful eye on us. 'It's an officer alright, Fred.'

Fred immediately lowered his rifle and walked over to us. 'I'm bloody glad to meet you, sir. We've been wandering around in this mist for some time. You're the first people we've seen. Have you any idea where we are?'

'Oh yes, I know where you are alright,' replied Jack. 'But explaining it to you is another thing. If you and your friend would care to follow us, we will get you out of here.' I turned and looked towards Harry. His eyes looked upwards, as if to say, 'Thank God, that's over.'

'Right then,' said Jack, 'if everyone is ready, we will go.' Jack took the lead. We slowly edged our way back to the meeting area. The further we came away from the fighting, the clearer the conditions became. We were the first ones to arrive back.

'Where are we?' asked Fred. 'I think you and your friend had better sit down,' answered Jack. 'I have something to say to you that will surprise you.'

The two soldiers found a place to sit and placed their rifles firmly across their knees. I looked across at the two of them and read the pain and fear that was deep inside them. They awaited their surprise with apprehension.

'Now that you have made yourselves comfortable,' said Jack, 'I will begin. Has it not seemed strange to you that you have found yourselves in this mist and that you have not seen anyone else except us?' 'Yes,' answered Fred. 'But what has that got to do with where we are now?' 'Well,' said Jack, 'how did you find yourself in this mist?' Fred turned to George: 'I don't really know. Do you, George?'

'It's strange,' said George. 'I remember we came under attack from the woods we were passing. I thought I took one in the head. I fell but woke up in this mist. My rifle lay next to me so I grabbed it as I stood up. I felt a strange sensation as if my body were not my own. This soon cleared. I could not quite make out where I was because of the mist and thought it best to find my platoon. That's when I came across you, Fred.' 'Yes, that's about what happened to me,' echoed Fred. 'Wait a moment. What's all this about, sir?'

Jack paused. I did not think he would be able to tell them that they were dead, but he plucked up the courage. With raised eyebrows he began: 'Well, gentlemen. The two of you have had your last battle. There will be no more fighting because you both died from the wounds you described.'

Before Jack could utter another word, the two soldiers were on their feet with their guns firmly in their hands. They looked at Jack as if he'd gone off his head.

'Look,' said George, 'we may not know quite where we are, or what has happened to us, but we know we're not dead. By the way, sir, that's an unusual uniform you have on. It's not one I'm familiar with. Have you seen it before, Fred?' 'No, I haven't,' replied Fred. 'They're not from our regiment, that's for certain. They could be Germans dressed up in our togs.' Once again the two soldiers raised their rifles at us. 'Can you tell us who you are, sir, and what regiment you're from?' George asked.

'Look here,' said Jack, 'you're dead and so are my two friends. As a matter of fact, we are all dead to the earth world. You're not helping things by pointing those guns at us. They will serve you no purpose here. If you wish to know who we are, I will tell you. My name is Captain Jack Purvis, my friend to your right is Sergeant Harry Willmott, and to your left, Private James Legget. We are all soldiers, but not from your war. We are from the Great War, where we died for King and country. Like yourselves, it was hard at first to comprehend we were dead, but it soon became apparent we were!'

'Look here, sir,' said George sympathetically. 'I think you had a whack on the head that has sent you a little barmy. Perhaps we can help you find one of the dressing stations, if you like. Sorry I was a bit short with you, but this confounded mist is enough to make anyone nervy.'

Harry cut George short. 'I will prove to you that you're dead. Point your rifle at me.' 'Now look,' said George, 'we've had enough of this nonsense. I just want to get back to our unit.

Please will you direct us?' 'Look,' said Harry, 'I want to prove to you I am dead. The only way to prove this is for you to shoot me. It will have no real effect on me because I can't die twice.'

'I'm sorry, friend,' said George, 'I'm not going to deliberately murder one of our own men. Fighting this darn war is my job. We've seen enough of our men butchered by the Nazis. Killing them is all I want to get on with.'

George paused for a minute, rubbed his head and said: 'I think the three of you have some sort of plan up your sleeve. Yes, that's it. You want to get back to Blighty by making out you're shellshocked. That's a good 'un.'

'No,' cried Harry. 'That's not right. We are telling you the truth, and I am trying to prove it. Please just point your rifle at my shoulder and fire. I promise there will be no comeback on you. Now, hurry up. I want you to see the results.' By this time George had become agitated. 'Bloody do it,' cried out Fred, 'so we can get out of here.'

'Right! Don't cry to me when it hurts,' shouted George. He pointed his rifle at Harry's shoulder and fired. It threw Harry backwards. A hole the size of a penny appeared in his shoulder, and blood poured from the wound. He lay groaning on the ground. On realizing what he had done, George flung his rifle to the ground and rushed over to Harry. There was a slight grin on George's face, as if to say, 'I told you so.' Slowly the grin faded from his face as we watched the severed edges of the wound knit together until there was no sign of Harry's having been shot.

'My God, it's healed itself,' cried George. 'Are you satisfied now?' I asked. 'I'm going off my head,' said George. 'This can't be happening. Fred, did you see what happened?' 'Yes, I bloody well did,' he said in a tone that suggested he didn't know if he was coming or going. 'What in hell is happening to us?' he asked.

Harry climbed back to his feet. When he had fully recovered, he stepped forward to where Fred stood. He looked him straight in the eye and said: 'You're not in hell yet, mate. But, if you don't take notice of us, you will surely drift there. As to being off your head, no you're not. But you are dead. Well, dead to the world you used to know. You have seen for yourselves what happened when you shot me. If you would like to look at my shoulder, you will see there is no evidence of my having been hurt at all.'

The two soldiers just stood there with their mouths open. I saw tears in the eyes of one of them. It's quite a blow when you first realize you are dead. 'What happens to us now?' Fred asked. Jack answered, 'We will wait here until some of our friends arrive. You will then be taken to a place where you can rest and adjust to your new home.'

While we waited, we took the opportunity to explain our work, hopefully in an understandable way. We also spoke about life on the astral plane. However, shock began to affect them. Fred paced up and down. He stopped every now and then to mutter something to himself. 'I'm not to see my wife and kids anymore,' he whispered. 'What will they do without me? No father to bring them up. They will have to fight for a miserable pension. How could this happen to me? How could it?' 'Will you shut up?' shouted George. 'Your whining is driving me mad. Just shut up.'

Tempers were becoming frayed. I did my best to calm them but had little success. Suddenly Captain Marsh appeared out of the mist and asked: 'Now, what's all this about?' Fred immediately began his story but was cut short by the captain. 'Quite right,' he said, 'those bloody bureaucrats have it all their own way. It's left to the likes of us to fight their wars, but there is nothing we can do by arguing. So let's have no more of this nonsense.'

'Sorry,' said Fred, and he gave a quick salute. 'Right then, lads,' said the officer. 'You will no longer require your rifles. You can throw them away. That's good.' As soon as they had thrown away their weapons, we made tracks out of the region. We headed towards the halfway house for lost souls. This particular building was different from the one I had gone to, but the organization was the same throughout the lower astral plane.

14

We left George and Fred in the charge of a sergeant and made
our way back into the mist. Before we got very far we came
across some of our group. They too had been successful. We
did not stop to talk but continued on our way. I turned to
Harry and said: 'That was some chance you took in being
shot.' 'Not really,' he said. 'I can tell you one thing, though, I
was bloody afraid. We were told to use our imagination. The
pain didn't matter. All I cared about was proving a point, but, I
don't mind telling you, it hurt.'

'Yes, well done,' said the officer. 'You used your initiative.
That's the way. All of you have done extremely well. And, the
more of this type of rescue you do, the more efficient you will
become. I must go back to headquarters. I will leave you
gentlemen to carry on.' The captain was soon out of sight.

'Which way shall we go this time?' enquired Harry. 'What
do you think, Jim?' Jack asked. 'This time,' I replied, 'let's go in
the other direction.'

We walked back into the mist. Occasionally there was an
opening in the mist which we used to get our bearings. We
wandered around for some time until we spotted another
clearing, which we entered. We made out the outline of a
building. When we looked more closely, we saw other buildings. We had stumbled on a farm. The farmhouse had been
under attack because all the windows at the front were
damaged. We approached with great care knowing it might be

occupied either by our chaps or by the enemy. We stopped some yards away to assess the situation. It looked deserted; there was no sign of movement. 'Do we go in or do we bypass it?' Jack asked.

We were discussing amongst ourselves when I got the feeling we were being watched. The feeling became stronger when I tried to shake it off. I had to say something about it. I was the only one to sense it, but we acted on it by taking a closer look at the house. We approached it rather gingerly. I saw a small face peering from the corner of one of the windows. Whoever it was realized they had been seen and disappeared quickly.

I shouted, 'Come on out. We mean you no harm. We just want to talk to you.' We waited for an answer, but none came. Suddenly the silence was broken by a loud crack. There was another and another. We didn't have to be clever to realize we were being shot at. Whoever was firing the weapon was not very accurate. We pulled back to plan the best way into the house. We knew we must materialize ourselves there. We also knew this method might shock the souls if they sighted us. It was a chance we would have to take. The three of us linked hands. Within moments we were in the house.

The room was sparse, except for several large boxes piled near the window. I noticed movement from behind the boxes. 'Look out!' I shouted and pushed Jack to the floor just in time. There was a loud crack, and a bullet whizzed past our heads. There was no time to think. Harry rushed towards the boxes and dived in. We heard a fierce struggle going on. Jack and I pulled ourselves to our feet and rushed over to give a hand. Before we could reach him, Harry gave out an enormous laugh and said, 'Well, I'll be ...'

'You all right, Harry?' I asked. 'Yes, thank you,' he said. 'Look what we have here.' Harry stepped from behind the boxes. In one hand he held a struggling young boy by the scruff of the neck, and in the other a rifle. 'That's mine,' cried the boy in broken English. 'Give it back to me.'

'You just wait a minute, lad,' replied Harry. 'We're not going to hurt you. We only want to talk to you. Calm down.' Jack went over to talk to the boy. There was another violent struggle. The lad gave Jack an almighty kick in the shin. 'That bloody hurt,' cried Jack. 'I ought to give you a clip around the ear for that.' I interrupted because I felt the tension rising: 'Jack, let me have a word with him.' Harry still held the boy in a vice-like grip and was not going to let go.

'Now son, what's your name?' I asked. 'Pierre,' he replied. 'Look, Pierre, we mean you no harm. Are you alone?' I asked. 'Yes,' he said. I had the feeling he was not telling the truth, but I thought it best not to say so. 'Pierre,' I continued, 'if my friend lets you go, will you promise not to run away?' He gave Harry a look that would have turned most men to stone. He then turned to me and looked into my eyes. I sensed the fear in him, but I knew I had to react differently to him than I had to John. 'Well, what's it to be?' I asked.

'I promise not to run away, but tell this one to take his hands off me.' 'Right, Harry, I think we can trust him,' I said. Harry let go. 'My gun, I want it. Give it to me,' cried Pierre. 'No,' I said, 'you don't need it anymore.'

'Are you Nazis?' he asked. 'Are you going to kill me like you did my Mama and Papa?' 'No, we are not Nazis,' I said. 'Look at our uniforms. We are British soldiers. If we were Nazis, we would have shot you by now. We are here to help you.' 'It's too late to help me,' he said. 'My family's gone.' Tears trickled down his cheeks as he explained about their deaths.

'To help you,' I said, 'we must take you to a place of safety.' 'No,' he cried. 'I'm not leaving here, not without...' He stopped abruptly. 'You're not leaving without whom?' I asked. 'Nobody,' he replied. 'I just want to be left on my own. that's all.'

Jack turned to me and asked, 'Do you think there are others here?' There was an immediate reaction from Pierre: 'No, I am alone,' he cried. 'Look, Pierre,' I said. 'I know there are others here. You are hiding them. Believe me, we mean you no harm.'

'If you are British soldiers,' he said, 'why are you here? We are occupied by the Nazis, not the British. You are probably German spies. That's it—Germans dressed in British uniforms.' 'I'm no bloody German,' remarked Harry. 'As to our being spies, take a good look at us. Our mission is to help those, such as yourself, in occupied countries. We don't have a lot of time. If you want our help, you had better make up your mind.'

I saw the approach Harry was taking and joined in: 'Yes, our orders are to find as many young partisans as possible. They will be trained as freedom fighters.' These words had a positive effect on Pierre. He chirped up, 'Will you help me fight the Nazis?' 'Yes,' I said, 'we will teach you how to become a freedom fighter.' My thoughts were of freedom for those oppressed by war. The weapon would be the will, not the gun. 'Good,' he said. 'I will come with you. First follow me.'

He led us into another room and pulled back a small carpet revealing a trap door. 'Wait here,' he said and raised the door. He disappeared down some steps. Jack tapped me on the shoulder: 'What are we going to do with them now? He will expect us to teach him to fight. Who knows how many of them are down there.'

'Wait, I have an idea,' said Harry. 'Why not give Captain Marsh a shout? Perhaps he can help.' 'That's a good idea,' I said. 'What do you think, Jack?' 'It could be the answer,' he replied. 'I will try to contact him.' Jack shut his eyes and concentrated for a short while. Suddenly, the silence was broken by the sound of feet on the steps. The noise broke Jack's concentration, and he was back with us.

'Did you manage to contact him?' I asked. 'Yes,' he replied. 'He's doing what he can to find Pierre's parents. He has asked me to touch Pierre's head for a minute or so. He will then be able to link with Pierre's vibration. When he has tuned into him, he will know all about him. Also, hopefully, from this contact, he will be able to find Pierre's family.'

Pierre lifted himself out of the opening in the floor and said, 'We come now.' He knelt down and pulled out two smaller boys, fussing over them for a moment or so. 'These are my brothers,' he said. 'When Papa died I became the man of the house. We had near misses with the Nazis, but they never got us.' Little does he realize, I thought.

'Come over here, Pierre,' called Jack. Pierre went over to where Jack stood. 'Now then,' continued Jack, 'I want you to stand to attention like a good soldier.' This pleased Pierre; he stood like a statue. 'I want to check your head size,' said Jack. 'It's important for a good soldier to have the right size beret. It must hold the badge of his battalion. We in the British army consider this an honour.'

I could not help but chuckle to myself and think that now

I'd heard it all. But it gave Jack an opportunity to place his hands on Pierre's head. Captain Marsh had plenty of time to gain the required information. 'Right, Private Pierre,' said Jack, 'get your brothers and follow us.' We left the house and stopped outside for Jack to make sure everyone was together.

'Where has all this mist come from?' enquired Pierre. 'I remember when the sun used to shine. It was always so clear, never this mist. One day I woke and found everything covered by it.' Harry was quick off the mark, replying, 'You're right. It's a new weapon the Nazis invented.' Pierre accepted the explanation, temporarily anyway. We journeyed back to the meeting area. I found the captain and explained what had happened. 'We will hold them here,' said Captain Marsh. 'We are still trying to locate their parents.'

'Right,' I answered and went back to the group. I called Harry and Jack to one side and explained the situation. 'We will have to keep them occupied until the captain sorts something out,' I said.

We returned to the children, and I started a conversation with Pierre. 'Do you believe in God?' I asked. 'But, of course,' he said. 'Does not everyone? Please, can you tell me why these soldiers walk around without guns? Is it not dangerous? How do we defend ourselves if we come under attack?' 'It's quite safe here,' I said. 'You will not need a gun. Anyway, we will not come under attack. Tell me, Pierre, what happened to your parents?'

'The Nazis shot them with the rest of the villagers. My brothers and I hid. I was so angry I ran back to my home and got Papa's gun. My two brothers came with me. We hid until dark. I found a good place to ambush the soldiers who killed returned my attention to the laughing boys and asked, 'Have you finished yet?'

'Oh, you tommies are so funny,' cried Pierre. I saw the smile on Pierre's face disappear, and I looked to where he was looking. Coming our way were an officer and two others. 'Well, here we go,' I told myself. The laughter died completely. Pierre let out a scream: 'No. It's not them. It can't be them.' Slowly Pierre got to his feet and walked towards the approaching figures. What started as a slow walk soon became a run. His two brothers followed close behind. I waited to see the outcome and hoped the reunion would not be too dramatic for them.

Captain Marsh beckoned me over. It was a sight to behold. The three lads held on to their mother, and the father wrapped his arms around all of them. Once again a family was reunited after death. The officer and I stepped to one side and exchanged a few words. He told me the family would be looked after. I decided not to interrupt the reunion and left them to rejoice together.

I walked over to Harry and Jack. The three of us returned to the mist. Our work continued throughout the war and beyond. The end of the war only meant there were no more souls coming to this side of life before their allotted time. We still had to help those who had died and were lost because of the war's complications. Even as I speak to you, Jack and Harry are working. We have come a long way since the early days, but our work continues. As long as man is inhuman to his brothers, we shall be needed.

ALSO FROM CLAIRVIEW

AND THE WOLVES HOWLED
Fragments of two lifetimes
Barbro Karlén

'An extraordinary book ... deserves to be taken seriously.'
—*International Herald Tribune..*

'... A very thought-provoking read! Whether or not she was really Anne Frank in another life, I do not doubt Karlén's sincerity.'
—Rabbi Yonassan Gershom, author of *Beyond the Ashes and From Ashes to Healing.*

For as long as she can remember, Barbro Karlén has harboured terrible memories of a previous existence on earth as the Jewish girl Anne Frank, author of the famous *Diary*. Until recently, she had kept this knowledge private. Now, prompted by a series of events which culminated in a struggle for her survival, she is ready to tell her amazing story.

   And the Wolves Howled is the autobiography of Barbro Karlén, from her early fame as a bestselling child literary sensation in her native Sweden, to her years as a policewoman and a successful dressage rider. But this is no ordinary life history. As the victim of discrimination, personal vendettas, media assassination, libel and attempted murder, Karlén is forced to fight for her very being. In the dramatic conclusion to her living nightmare, she is shown the karmic background to these events. She glimpses fragments of her former life, and begins to understand how forces of destiny reach over from the past into the present. With this knowledge she is finally free to be herself...

£10.95; 272pp (8 b/w plates); ISBN 1 902636 18 X

PSYCHIC WARRIOR
The true story of the CIA's paranormal espionage
programme
David Morehouse

When David Morehouse—a much decorated army officer—was hit by
a stray bullet, he began to be plagued with visions and uncontrolled
out-of-body experiences. As a consequence, he was recruited as a
psychic spy for STARGATE, a highly-classified programme of
espionage instigated by the CIA and the US Defence Department.
Trained to develop spiritual, clairvoyant capacities, he became one
of a select band of 'remote viewers' in pursuit of previously unat-
tainable political and military secrets.

When Morehouse discovered that the next step in the top-secret
programme was 'remote influencing'—turning 'viewers' like himself
into deadly weapons—he rebelled. In his efforts to expose the programme, he and his family endured the full force of the US intelli-
gence community's attempts to silence him. As the multi-million-
dollar STARGATE scandal was exposed to the world, Morehouse
himself became the enemy of the secret services...

In *Psychic Warrior*, one of STARGATE's 'viewers' finally reveals the
extraordinary truth of this secret operation.

£9.95; 280pp (8 b/w plates); ISBN 1 902636 20 1

MY DESCENT INTO DEATH
and the message of love which brought me back
Howard Storm

'For twenty years, I have been listening to and reading innumerable accounts of near-death experiences, but I have rarely encountered one as powerful as Howard Storm's'–Dr Kenneth Ring, author of *Lessons from the Light*.

'... I consider Howard Storm's near death experience one of the greatest that I am aware of ... I highly recommend this book.'–George Ritchie, author of *Return from Tomorrow* and *Ordered to Return*.

For years Howard Storm lived the American dream. He had a fine home, a family, and a successful career as an art professor and painter. Then, without warning, he found himself in hospital in excruciating pain, awaiting an emergency operation. He realized with horror that his death was a real possibility.

Storm was totally unprepared for what was to happen next. He found himself out of his body, staring at his own physical form. But this was no hallucination; he was fully aware and felt more alive than ever before. In his spirit form, Storm was drawn into fearsome realms of darkness and death, where he experienced the terrible consequences of a life of selfishness and materialism. However, his journey also took him into regions of light where he conversed with angelic beings and the Lord of Light Himself, who sent him back to earth with a message of love.

My Descent into Death is Howard Storm's full story: from his near death experience in Paris to his full recovery back home in the United States, and the subsequent transformation of his life. Storm also communicates what he learned in his conversations with heavenly spiritual beings, revealing how the world will be in the future, the real meaning of life, what happens when we die, the role of angels, and much more. What he has to say will challenge those who believe that human awareness ends with death.

£8.95; 184pp (8 b/w plates); 1 902636 16 3

LIGHT BEYOND THE DARKNESS
How I healed my suicide son after his death
Doré Deverell

'This book is the best I have ever seen for people who have suffered through having a member of their family committing suicide.'– George Ritchie, author of *Return from Tomorrow* and *Ordered to Return*.

Doré Deverell's son Richard had led a difficult life, plagued by physical and mental illness and depression. When he committed suicide at the age of 36, Doré was naturally devastated, suffering the intense anguish of a mother's loss. But she was determined to search for healing and reconciliation.

This book is the first-hand account of how Doré Deverell made contact with Richard after his death. Encountering the work of the spiritual teacher Rudolf Steiner, she discovered unique methods by which she could communicate with her son's spirit. Suicides, she learned, often experience great suffering and regret as a consequence of their premature death. But Doré was taught how to help alleviate Richard's pain, and finally metamorphose it. These practical steps are described in an accessible way to aid anybody who finds themselves in a similar tragic situation.

In the unexpected conclusion to this extraordinary tale, Doré finds the person who, she believes, embodies Richard's reincarnated soul. Her work is rewarded with new hope, and Richard's soul is given a chance to learn and develop on earth once again.

Light Beyond the Darkness is a gripping account of love, despair, death and resurrection. Its central message–that, through the spirit, light overcomes dark–is a heartwarming confirmation of spiritual reality.

£8.95; 144pp; 1 902636 19 8